ALEXANDER
THE
GREAT

NICK SEKUNDA AND JOHN WARRY

OSPREY
PUBLISHING

First published in Great Britain in 2004 by Osprey Publishing, Elms Court, Chapel Way, Botley, Oxford OX2 9LP, United Kingdom.
Email: info@ospreypublishing.com

© 2004 Osprey Publishing Ltd.

A CIP catalogue record for this book is available from the British Library

ISBN 1 84176 893 6

Editor: Iain MacGregor
Design: Mike Moule
Colour bird's-eye views by Cilla Eurich
Maps by Micromap
Artwork by Angus McBride and Richard Geiger
Wargaming Alexander's Campaigns by Arthur Harman
Filmset in Singapore by Pica Ltd
Printed in China through World Print Ltd.

04 05 06 07 08   10 9 8 7 6 5 4 3 2 1

For a catalog of all books published by Osprey Military and Aviation please contact:

Osprey Direct USA, c/o MBI Publishing, P.O. Box 1, 729 Prospect Ave, Osceola, WI 54020, USA
E-mail: info@ospreydirectusa.com

Osprey Direct UK, P.O. Box 140, Wellingborough, Northants, NN8 2FA, UK
E-mail: info@ospreydirect.co.uk

www.ospreypublishing.com

FRONT COVER Alexander the Great, King of Macedonia, Pella 356 BC - Babylon 323 BC. Herm bust, sculpture, copy after Lysippus. Marble, height 68 cm. Paris, Musee du Louvre. Photo: akg-images, London/ Erich Lessing.

KEY TO MILITARY SYMBOLS

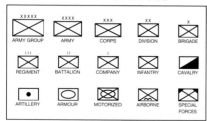

CONTENTS

BOOK 1

ALEXANDER'S ARMY

The Army of Alexander the Great

Introduction

The figures of Napoleon and Alexander stand comparison: both were supremely successful generals, both were short of stature, both dreamed of world conquest, both covered up their failures, and both came to be virtually worshipped. The same comparison cannot be made of the modern literature dealing with their armies. There are books dealing with Alexander's principal battles and campaigns, books dealing with his generalship and with limited aspects of the army, but no book dealing with the army as such.

The reasons for this are not hard to find. We only know the details of Alexander's reign from a small number of works written some centuries after the events they describe. These frequently contradict one another, and in many cases they can be shown to contain obvious errors. The patient work of scores of scholars over the last century has advanced our knowledge of the details of the Macedonian army immeasurably and, although many problems still defy solution, we have perhaps reached a position now where such a book can be attempted.

A monograph of this size cannot pretend to fill the gap. Almost every statement in the text below could be challenged. Lack of space has made it impossible to credit the work of previous scholars and the individual suggestions they have made to resolve particular problems; but it is hoped that the debate can be followed through the pages of the books mentioned under 'Further Reading'. Conversely, some new suggestions have been advanced in the text, but again lack of space has prevented me from defending them in full detail. I have also limited my subject to the army down to the end of 331 BC, though I have dealt with the later reforms in outline, and I have continued some of the unit histories beyond that date. So while this book does not attempt a comprehensive treatment, it is offered as an introduction to Alexander's army.

What brings the events of 2,300 years ago to life more than anything else is the vivid picture we create in our mind's eye of the glorious struggle described in the texts, so this book concentrates on giving an idea of how the regiments of the army were uniformed. Two archaeological sources are of inestimable value. The Alexander Mosaic is a Roman copy of a contemporary painting, possibly an apotheosis-painting of Alexander in battle against the Persians by Apelles. Colour reproductions occur in most illustrated books on Alexander. The Alexander Sarcophagus, commissioned by Alexander's vassal King Abdalonymus of Sidon and now in the Archaeological Museum, Istanbul, is not so accessible to the general reader. The once-vivid paint which originally adorned the figures was already greatly faded when the

A gold medallion showing the head of Philip of Macedon, from a hoard of such pieces, featuring various members of the royal house, dating from the Roman period—mid-3rd century AD—and recovered at Tarsus in the last century. Recent reconstruction from the partially cremated skull found in Philip's tomb at Vergina demonstrated that his right eye had been destroyed, with massive tissue damage to the socket. Ancient sources tell us that the king's eye was shot out during the siege of Methone. (Bibliothèque Nationale, Paris)

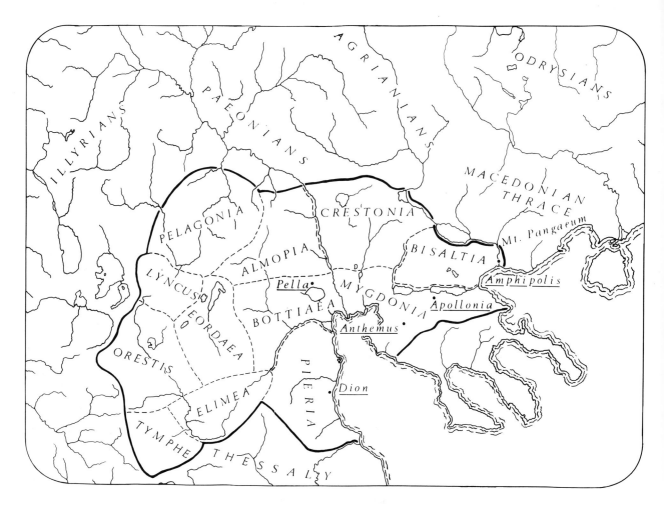

sarcophagus was excavated nearly a century ago. The paint faded rapidly on excavation and progressively thereafter. The original publication of O. Hamdy Bey and Theodore Reinach—*Une nécropole royale à Sidon* (Paris 1892)—included some heliochromes of the Sarcophagus which, despite their generally poor quality, add some details to the magnificently complete *Der Alexandersarkophag aus Sidon* (Strassburg 1912) of F. Winter. Both these books are extremely rare, and can only be found in a very few libraries in this country. Some further information can be gleaned from G. Mendel's Catalogue of Sculptures in the Museum (although this information has to be treated with some caution); and from Volkmar von Graeve's *Der Alexandersarkophag und seine Werkstatt* (Berlin 1970), which uses special photography to add details of the faded paint not now visible, and is most useful for its complete notes. Finally, some problems of contradictory information have been resolved (and some guesses made) from personal observations

made in Istanbul, and I would like to take this opportunity to thank the Museum authorities and friends in Istanbul for their help and time given under difficult circumstances.

Philip's Army

When Philip II ascended the throne at the age of 23 in 359 BC, Macedonia was in danger of being engulfed by wild barbarian tribes to the north and wily Greek cities to the south. They exploited her internal weaknesses: there were other pretenders to the throne, and authority could be exerted over the semi-independent principalities of Upper Macedonia only intermittently. Philip had to expand the power of the throne or be swallowed up by the difficulties surrounding him: the creation of a powerful army was imperative.

Philip dealt with the northern tribes first. Like his

own army, these tribal levies were but lightly equipped—peltasts armed with javelins and light shields (*peltai*). Philip re-armed his infantry, composed of peasant levies—all healthy male subjects of the king were liable for service—with longer, heavier fighting spears; and issued them with some light armour, borrowing the ideas of the Athenian general Iphicrates, who had been campaigning in the area shortly beforehand. This new force of infantry was toughened up by long training marches under the summer sun, and mercenary generals were brought in to impose discipline and instruct in drill. The northern tribesmen were dealt with by this improvised force of infantry; but a showdown with the armies of Greece was inevitable, and his infantry needed to be much better equipped to stand up to the Greek hoplites.

Greek battles had been decided up to now by the manoeuvres of heavy infantry, the hoplites, who had become increasingly lightly equipped during the 4th century, abandoning much of their armour. This enabled them to execute their tactical evolutions on the battlefield with speed and without too much fatigue.

Philip, however, created a large force of heavily-equipped cavalry to act as the *corps de rupture* of his army. At first he had only about 600 Companion cavalrymen. Noble families from all over the Greek world were settled on fiefs created out of lands won from the king's enemies, and by the end of his reign their number had been multiplied many times over. Philip gave them heavy armour—cuirasses and helmets of the 'Phrygian' type—and he further developed the new tactical formations Jason of Pherai had invented to enable his cavalry to take a leading role in battle. The infantry no longer needed its mobility.

Philip consolidated his hold on the rich mines of Pangaeum, which yielded 1,000 talents annually, and re-equipped his infantry with the bronze hoplite shields and cuirasses which had been abandoned in the rest of Greece for more than half a century. Thus, when the final showdown came in 338 BC at Chaeronea, the Greek hoplites smashed themselves to pieces against the solid lines of the more heavily-equipped Macedonian phalanx. An unwilling Greece was united under Philip in the League of Corinth; but the king was assassinated at

A relief from Pelinna in Thessaly: the cloak identifies this horseman as a Macedonian, while the 'Phrygian' helmet is very similar to that found in the Vergina tomb. The artist has omitted reins, horse-furniture and boots. Note that the rider is shown clean-shaven. (Louvre, Paris)

the age of 46 before he could launch his planned expedition against the Persian Empire.

The first year of Alexander's reign was taken up in re-establishing his hold on Greece and the Balkans, but he found time to introduce some changes in the army. He introduced stave-fighting into the training programme, and in the cavalry he replaced the 'Phrygian' helmet with the Boeotian, which gave more protection to the face and shoulders against sword-cuts. He also ordered the army to shave, officially to deny the enemy a hand-hold in close combat. Shaving was only just becoming popular in Greece and many of the older members of the court refused to rid themselves of their curly beards. Looking at busts of the new king, who had just turned 20, one wonders if he had any need to obey the regulation himself.

PRINCIPAL DATES IN THE REIGNS OF PHILIP AND ALEXANDER

359	Philip becomes king.
356	Alexander born.
338	?2 August: Battle of Chaeronea.
336	Spring: Expeditionary force sent to Asia, withdrawn on death of Philip(?)
	Summer: Alexander becomes king.

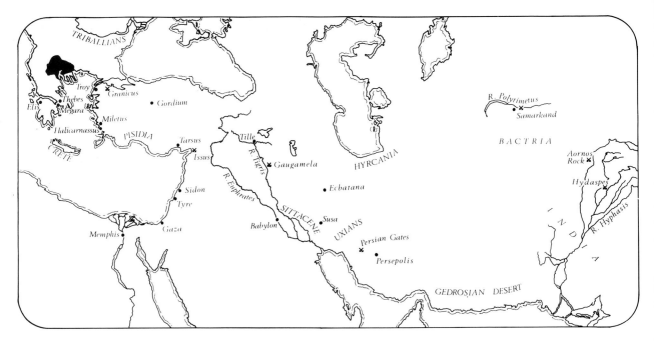

335	Spring: Balkan Campaigns. Destruction of Thebes.
334	Spring: Expeditionary force crosses Hellespont. May: Battle of Granicus. Sieges of Miletus and Halicarnassus.
334/3	Winter campaign in Pisidia.
333	Reinforcements reach army at Gordium. September/October: Battle of Issus.
332	Siege of Tyre. Siege of Gaza.
332/1	Reinforcements reach army in Memphis and Syria.
331	?30 September: Battle of Gaugamela. ?November: Army re-forms in Sittacene. Campaign against the Uxians.
330	Late January: Storming of Persian Gates. ?June–July: Greek allies dismissed at Ecbatana; pursuit of Darius. Hyrcanian Campaign.
329	Operations near Samarkand; massacre at the River Polytimetus.
327/6	Capture of Aornos Rock.
326	Indian campaign begins. Battle of Hydaspes. Mutiny on the Hyphasis.
325	March through Gedrosian Desert.
323	10/11 June: Alexander dies.

The Court

The army, like the state, was run from the court which always travelled with the king. This comprised a hundred or so courtiers, called 'Personal Companions' (*hoi amph' auton hetairoi*) or sometimes simply 'Companions' (*hetairoi*) in the texts. These Companions should not be confused with the Companion Cavalry; 'Companion' is simply a court title. Thus when we hear of a Companion being appointed to command such-and-such a unit, the man in question should be considered a Personal Companion. Similarly, when we hear of Alexander addressing a council of Companions we should understand that the young king has assembled a small group of his courtiers, not a democratic assembly of the Companion Cavalry. Our sources also refer to the king's 'Friends' (*philoi*), a term for courtier current in Hellenistic times. It could refer to the highest grade of Personal Companion at court, but it could also be an anachronism, simply equating with Personal Companion. In battle the Personal Companions fought alongside the king in the Royal Squadron of the Companion Cavalry.

One figure on the Alexander Sarcophagus wears a purple Macedonian cloak with a yellow border (see Plate B3). In Hellenistic times the king would give his courtiers purple cloaks as a mark of their rank, so it seems that the practice was already established in Alexander's reign, the figure representing a Personal Companion. After the battle of Issus, Alexander sends Leonnatus to inform the Persian royal family that Darius has not died; Diodorus describes Leonnatus as one of the Friends while Curtius terms him *ex purpuratis*. Alexander sometimes wore 'fancy dress' in his battles, but he normally dressed in the uniform of an officer of the Companion Cavalry. He is dressed as such on the Alexander Mosaic (see Plate A1), but he wears the purple cloak of a Personal Companion and not the regimental cloak. The edge of the cloak is destroyed on the mosaic, but the border is clearly shown on some of the bronze statuettes representing Alexander. Our sources mention the royal trappings worn by the king's horse; perhaps these may be the elaborate metal harness ornaments shown on the mosaic.

The king ran the army from the royal tent. This seems to have been an impressive pavilion, with a large chamber where the council of war met (perhaps separate from the main tent); a vestibule beyond, which none could enter without passing Chares the royal usher (*eisangeleus*); the armoury (perhaps also separate from the main tent); and the king's apartments, in which he bathed, and slept, beyond the vestibule. It was court custom for all to remove their headdress when addressing the king. The tent was dug in and erected by its own work-party, commanded by a Macedonian called Proxenus. The person of the king was ministered to by his chamberlains (*rhabdophoroi*, *rhabdouchoi*), or 'wand-carriers', the wand being their badge of office. These men accompanied the king when bathing, dressing, etc., and were selected both for their wit and their fidelity. The royal tent itself was guarded by a watch selected from the Bodyguards (*sōmatophylakes*) on a rota basis, while the area of the royal quarters was defended by a detachment of Hypaspists.

No Greek army was complete without a 'chaplains' department', whose job it was to provide favourable omens by augury to satisfy the suspicious soldiery. Aristander the seer performed this role with considerable aplomb, but on occasion even Aristander needed a little help. A passage in Frontinus describes how Alexander, a self-styled divinity himself, used a special preparation to write 'victory is ordained for Alexander' on Aristander's hand before a sacrifice. During the ceremony the

This head of Alexander, originally from Alexandria and now in the British Museum, shows the young king at the age of 20—we are reminded that he ordered his army to shave off facial hair. (British Museum)

priest would put his hand under the victim's innards, and it would magically acquire the divine message to be shown to the gawping army. At the battle of Gaugamela an eagle was observed flying over the king. Our sources describe Aristander's dress, as he rode along the Macedonian line pointing out the omen, as consisting of white robes with a golden crown on his head (which we should understand to be a wreath of leaves worked in gold) and a laurel wreath in his right hand. Sacrificial knives took the shape of a small *kopis*.

The Royal Pages

It was a practice going back to Philip's time that the sons of the Macedonian nobility who had reached adolescence should be enrolled into the Royal Pages (*basilikoi paides*). At court these young men received

Roman bronze of Alexander: note the border shown on the king's cloak. (British Museum)

their education, and at the same time they served as a guarantee of their parents' loyalty. (Should any Macedonian be found guilty of treason, the custom was that the whole family involved should be wiped out root and branch.) No one had the power of chastising them by flogging except the king himself. The noble youths were given a general education in philosophy and the other liberal disciplines, but an emphasis was put on the more manly pursuits of hunting and *sphaira*—a violent ball game similar to rugby football.

The most important role of the institution, however, was to inculcate obedience to the king and deference to the king's majesty into the noble youth of Macedonia. Consequently they were called upon to perform duties not very different from those of slaves. They served on the king at table, stood guard at the doors of his bed-chamber and led in his concubines, poured the king's bath, prepared his dinner, and under the supervision of the royal chamberlains they performed all the menial functions required by the royal household.

They also accompanied the king out of doors. They received the horses from the grooms, led them up to the king and helped him mount. They may also have performed similar functions for the king's Personal Companions. We hear of an official called the 'Royal Groom' who seems to be a senior member of the Court entrusted with the care of the king's horses. They also looked after the king's armour, and accompanied him in the hunt.

Two mosaics from Pella show young men of the court at the hunt. They wear a narrow rectangular white cloak fastened with a brooch. In two cases the cloak has a red border and two of the young men wear white sun-hats: these are probably Royal Pages.

On leaving the Royal Pages the young men would either be trained as officers in the Royal Bodyguard, if they had proved themselves able, or they would enter the ranks of the aristocratic Companion Cavalry regiment.

The Bodyguards

Our sources frequently mention a Bodyguard (*sōmatophylakia*) or Bodyguards (*sōmatophylakes*); in Curtius they are called *armigeri* or *satellites*. These men are generally assumed to be a detachment of the Hypaspists detailed to guard the king. This is improbable, however, for in three separate passages (3.17.2, 4.3.2, 4.30.3) Arrian mentions that Alexander takes with him the Bodyguards *and* the Hypaspists. So it seems that the Bodyguard is a separate unit—and a unit of some strength, for in the third passage Arrian speaks of some 700 Bodyguards and Hypaspists. If we were to deduct a *lochos* of Hypaspists we would be left with a number of 200 or so for the Bodyguard. Nor was the unit one of insignificant status, for Alexander's close friend Hephaistion, who was appointed a brigadier in the Companion Cavalry in 330, commanded the Bodyguard at Gaugamela only a year earlier (Diodorus 17.61.3).

The most senior rank in the army was that of 'Royal Bodyguard' (*sōmatophylax basilikos*), the equivalent of *archisōmatophylax* in Hellenistic armies,

A relief from Troy showing Alexander: the horse-furniture has several interesting features, such as the buckle on the saddle girth. Note the figure on the left. The object held in the right hand does not seem to be a spear, since it is carried under the right arm: it could be a chamberlain's wand of office. (Museo Arqueologico Nacional, Madrid)

or of 'staff officer' in more modern armies. There were seven Royal Bodyguards, and this number was rigidly maintained. If a Royal Bodyguard were made satrap or died, another general was immediately promoted to take his place. The number seven was probably connected with the Bodyguards' original function of providing a daily watch to guard the king's tent. When Peucestas saved the king's life in India the number of Royal Bodyguards was changed to eight, as Alexander wanted to appoint him instantly as a mark of his gratitude. We frequently hear of a Royal Bodyguard being appointed to temporary command of a division of the army.

The Bodyguard itself seems to have been composed of young adult noblemen, for Diodorus (17.65.1) mentions that the army, when in Sittacene, was joined by 50 sons of the king's friends

sent by their fathers to serve as bodyguards. The equivalent passage in Curtius is rather confused, for he adds that the fifty sons were adults, but he then goes on to describe the duties of the Royal Pages—which these men would not perform if they were adult. Indeed, the man who brought this detachment from Macedonia, Amyntas son of Andromenes, later states, during his trial, that Alexander had sent him to Macedonia to fetch the 'many young men fit for service who were hidden away in your mother's palace'—so it seems that the 50 had already served as Royal Pages in Macedonia.

The Bodyguard, then, seems to have been composed of young men who had already served in the Royal Pages. They acted as personal bodyguards to the king and guarded his tent, but the Bodyguard probably also combined the functions of an officer training corps and a staff corps. They may have acted as aides to the Royal Bodyguards, but even if this were not the case they would certainly be at the centre of things and so would gain a good idea of how the army worked. I believe it is highly probable that the Macedonian officer corps had all seen service in the Bodyguard at one time or another. As we have already seen, however, from time to time the Bodyguard was called upon to fight as an active unit, so the young men would also gain some practical experience of soldiering.

The Bodyguards seem to be distinguished by a distinctive uniform, for Amyntas is allowed to wear the dress of a Bodyguard during his trial. Unfortunately no further details are given (though see Plates E2, E3 and H2), but the Bodyguards do seem to use javelins in some places in the texts.

Command and Communications

The army Alexander took over to Asia in the spring of 334 BC was far from homogeneous. Its core was the army of the Kingdom of Macedonia itself, hereafter called the 'Royal Army'. Added to this were contingents supplied to the expeditionary force by the vassal princedoms on Macedonia's borders—Paeonians, Agrianians, Triballians, Odrysians and Illyrians. Alexander was also *archon* of

The mosaics of the royal palace at Pella frequently depict young men of the court, probably Royal Pages, in hunting scenes. They wear small cloaks, either white or white with red borders. (Pella Museum)

Trumpeter in the dress of a Thessalian cavalryman, drawn from a 5th century Corinthian vase in the National Museum, Athens.

Thessaly and so head of the Thessalian army. He was also head of the League of Corinth, which most of the states of Greece had been forced to join, and which supplied Alexander with contingents of infantry, cavalry and ships from their own armed forces. Finally, the numbers of the expeditionary force were augmented by a large number of mercenaries who were mostly Greeks, though some of Alexander's units of Balkan troops may have been mercenaries too.

The Greeks could not understand the strange patois of their language spoken by the Macedonians, and did not consider them to be Greek at all. To the Greeks they were uncouth, semi-civilised barbarians. The Macedonians for their part despised the Greeks as éffete, wishy-washy Greeklings. Both regarded the Thracians as scarcely capable of walking on their hind legs. It is a tribute to the leadership of the army that racial tensions were kept at such a low key. King Philip had once

Two examples of a rare silver *dekadrachm* showing Alexander in battle with Porus' elephants. The reverse shows Victory about to crown Alexander, who holds a thunderbolt. Both coins are very worn; but Alexander seems to wear a cuirass, a plumed and crested helmet of 'Phrygian' shape, and a peculiar type of cloak—perhaps an *ephaptis*? The king may be in the uniform of a senior officer of the Bodyguards. The lappets showing underneath the helmet may belong to a helmet liner: cf. Plate D1. (British Museum)

been wounded in rioting between his Macedonian soldiers and Greek mercenaries, and had only been able to escape by feigning death.

At its highest level the army was commanded by its staff officers, the 'Royal Bodyguards', and by the other generals (*stratēgoi*). The army would frequently be divided into a number of divisions (*moirai*), especially during the later campaigns, and a general would be appointed to command each. It was usual for these generals to retain direct command of an individual unit too, so many of the infantry *taxeis* were commanded by *stratēgoi*, not *taxiarchs*. Below the generals were the rest of the officers, the *hēgemones*, who were selected from the families of the Macedonian aristocracy. The officers were allowed their own baggage animals and servants and many, it seems, maintained their own 'train'. Command of individual units was very much a family affair. Many of the army units seem to be commanded by members of baronial families prominent in the area where they had been recruited. Perdiccas son of Orontes, who commands the *taxis* from Orestis, was of royal stock, probably from the ducal house of Orestis. The *taxis* of Amyntas son of Andromenes was commanded by his brother Simmias when Amyntas was back in Macedonia recruiting more troops, and another brother, Attalus, may have taken over command of the *taxis* after Amyntas' death. The Macedonian peasantry had to be commanded by men it respected. The 'new men' Philip had admitted into the ranks of the Companions were scarcely less noble, though not of vintage Macedonian stock. These men had to make do with less prestigious army commands. Thus we find the two sons of Larichus of Mitylene, Erigyius and Laomedon, both favourites of Alexander, making do with a brigade of Allied Horse and a commission in charge of the barbarian captives respectively.

Command was very centralised. The king himself would give the army its orders, down to such details as when to take breakfast. At first these were all given by trumpet signals. We hear of trumpet signals for the attack, the withdrawal, the call to arms, strike camp, march, ground arms and the alarm. The signal would be given first of all by Alexander's trumpeter, and then taken up by the trumpeters attached to each unit. It may be that at the lower levels the regimental trumpeters added a unit prefix to their trumpet signals, as is the case in modern armies. The day and the night were both divided into a number of watches, and it seems that the change of watch was signalled by trumpet, although this may be a detail of Roman military practice inserted into his narrative by Curtius. Similarly the frequent references to standards in Curtius are to be rejected as a Roman embellishment of the text.

Administration

The whole of Alexander's empire was run by a secretariat divided up into various sections (e.g. the Treasury), each, it seems, run by a Royal Secretary (*grammateus basilikos*). We can compare the 'Royal' Secretaries to the 'Royal' Bodyguards—both officers of the highest rank in the secretariat and the army. The Army Secretariat was under Eumenes of Cardia, who rose to prominence as one of the ablest of the warlords who disputed Alexander's empire after his death. Eumenes is once described as *archigrammateus* (chief secretary), but the title has a Hellenistic ring about it and it may be anachronistic.

The men who made up the Secretariat, though they might be able and even Personal Companions of the king, were usually men debarred by obscurity of birth or physical infirmity from holding a field command. These 'basest of men' were despised by the officers of the rest of the army. After Alexander's death Neoptolemus, the commander of the Hypaspists, was heard to remark that he had followed the king with his spear and shield, but Eumenes only with his escritoir.

The Army Secretariat was based in the tent of the Royal Secretary of the Army, which contained copies of all correspondence relevant to the army and all army documentation. The bases of army documentation were the muster-rolls (*syllogismous*) and conduct sheets (*syntelesas*), which gave the current strengths of the various units, and according to which pay and equipment, reinforcements, and on occasion rations were distributed and promotions were made. We hear of arms, armour, clothing, goblets and baggage-animals being issued in this way, on an occasional general issue basis rather than on a permanent one-for-one basis. Thus we should conclude that stores were not held at unit level but were held centrally in the baggage train.

When stores were distributed this was done by *lochoi* in the infantry and *ilai* in the cavalry (*hekatostuas* or 'hundreds' after 331). At company and squadron level it was then the duty of the *hypēretai*, or 'attendants', to allocate the stores further. We hear of these *hypēretai* only once in Diodorus (17.109.2), when the ringleaders of a mutiny are handed over to them for punishment. In Hellenistic times the *hypēretai* performed the duties of a modern sergeant-major. Responsible for matters concerning discipline and administration, he would maintain the muster-rolls and conduct sheets, and, in general, help the *lochagos* or *ilarch* run his command. Promoted from the ranks, we may imagine that his ultimate aspiration was to 'fly a desk' in the Army Secretariat.

The Army Secretariat was divided into various sections, each under a Secretary (*grammateus*) assisted by a number of Inspectors (*episkopoi*). We hear of a Secretary of Cavalry and a Secretary of Mercenaries for Egypt, who has two Inspectors under him. We also hear of Inspectors being detached from the main army to administer the military forces left in a province. The Secretary of Cavalry had the most difficult job, as one of his responsibilities was the procurement and distribution of remounts. Huge numbers of horses died in battle, and in an age before horseshoes a cavalry mount could easily be ruined by a long march. At the battle of Gaugamela the cavalry, 7,000 strong, lost a thousand mounts: nearly one in three of the Companion Cavalry lost theirs. Sequestration was used to obtain remounts locally, but more usually it was the duty of provincial governors to procure horses and despatch them to the remount pool. Many cities or provinces paid tribute on the hoof. In the last resort recourse had to be made to sequestration of surplus mounts within the army itself. We hear of an argument between the powerful nobleman Amyntas son of Andromenes

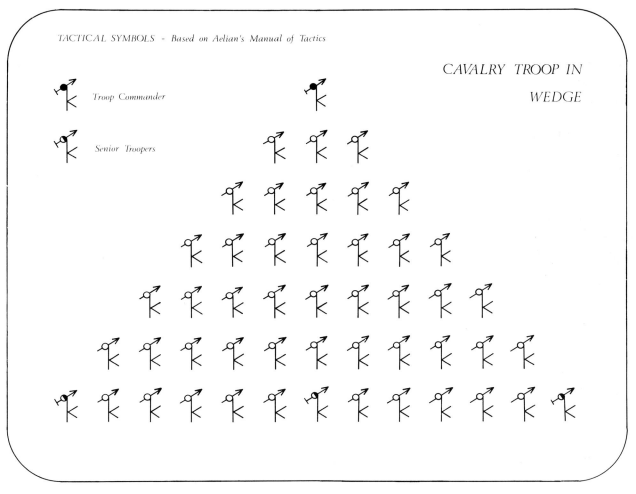

TACTICAL SYMBOLS - Based on Aelian's Manual of Tactics

CAVALRY TROOP IN WEDGE

Troop Commander

Senior Troopers

and Antiphanes the Secretary of Horse. Amyntas complains that Antiphanes, 'the basest of men', has taken eight out of the 10 horses he brought with him from Macedonia.

Rations were not generally issued. It was the responsibility of each soldier to purchase his own rations from the host of sutlers, frequently Phoenician traders, who followed the army. The local inhabitants of conquered territory were often obliged to provide markets for the soldiery when provisions were scarce. Sequestration was used in the last resort. If the army was about to cross barren areas, however, where the normal system would break down, rations were collected and held centrally in the baggage train, sealed with the Royal Seal, ready for emergency distribution.

The Cavalry

Organisation and Tactics

The building-block of the cavalry was the *ilē* (squadron) of 200 men, commanded by an *ilarch* and divided into four *tetrarchiai* of 49 men, each under the command of a *tetrarch*. The tactical formation adopted by the *tetrarchia* was the 'wedge', an invention of Philip, with the *tetrarch* at the point, and senior troopers riding in the middle and at each end of the 13-man base line. The *ilarch* was probably accompanied by a trumpeter to relay signals to the four troop commanders, and a *hypēretes* to help him administer the squadron. The four wedges would be drawn up in a squadron battle line with sufficient intervals in between each troop to ensure that each had space to manoeuvre, and none collided with each other in the charge (which frequently happens, because the frontage of each troop expands in the charge as the galloping horses try to move away from each other).

It was the battle-aim of Alexander to advance his army obliquely so as to cause dislocations in the Persian line as they attempted to outflank him on his right. The Persian cavalry column attempting to turn his right flank would be kept at bay by successive charges of his light cavalry, delivered squadron by squadron. As the Persian cavalry was forced to move further to the right, they would eventually lose contact with their main battle line.

As soon as this dislocation was observed in the Persian battle line, Alexander personally led the decisive charge of his heavy cavalry straight for it. None of this was possible until new cavalry formations were developed in the early 4th century: cavalry formations which allowed the squadrons to redeploy rapidly and reorient the axis of attack. The wedge gave this flexibility to Alexander's cavalry, which is vividly illustrated in Curtius' description of the cavalry fighting at Issus which took place when a massive Persian cavalry column charged the Thessalian cavalry.

'But on the right the Persians were strongly attacking the Thessalian horsemen, and

Head of a cavalryman from the Alexander Mosaic in Pompeii. The silvering of the Boeotian helmet, the golden wreath, and the white horsehair plume are probably all insignia of senior officer rank. (German Archaeological Institute, Rome)

already one squadron had been ridden down by their very onset, when the Thessalians, smartly wheeling their horses about, slipped aside and returning to the fray, with great slaughter, overthrew the barbarians, whom confidence in their victory has scattered and thrown into disorder.'

A number of *ilai*, usually two, three or four, might be formed into a cavalry brigade, or *hipparchy*, commanded by a *hipparch*. At first the number of squadrons per brigade was variable, but later on the

Two plaques of a large sculpted relief discovered in 1948 and now in the National Museum, Athens. Dating from Alexander's time or shortly afterwards, it shows a cavalry officer's horse with pantherskin shabraque. The groom, a black African slave, wears a short tunic and boots. Traces of a Boeotian helmet painted at the back of the relief can still be made out.

system became more standardised.

Each cavalryman was allowed a groom, who may have been mounted, to look after his horse and equipment. The grooms were stationed behind the squadron in battle. The cavalrymen owned their own horses, though it was customary for a man drafted into the cavalry to be granted an initial 'establishment' to enable him to purchase a mount of suitable quality. Horses lost in action were replaced from the army pool of remounts. Alexander and the rest of the cavalry normally marched on foot to spare the horses, as troopers have done throughout history, and the horses were left unbridled unless action was imminent. The Greeks used a very severe bit with spiked 'hedgehog' rollers, which could ruin the horse's delicate mouth if left bridled too long.

Cavalry Equipment

Alexander, it seems, replaced the 'Phrygian' helmet, probably painted in regimental colours, with the Boeotian helmet left plain bronze. The cavalry helmets on the Alexander Sarcophagus and the Pompeiian mosaic seem to show insignia of rank, as was normal Greek practice. One helmet on the mosaic is silvered, with a gold wreath and a horsehair 'tail' fixed on the crown; one helmet on the sarcophagus is plain bronze with a white or silver wreath, and a second helmet on the mosaic is

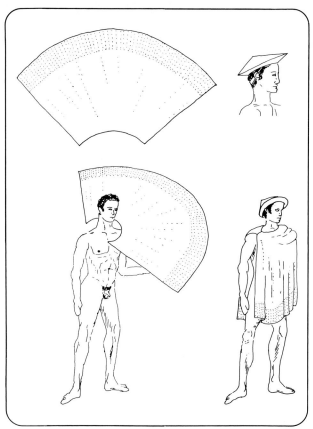

plain bronze with a white horsehair 'tail'. These could be the insignia of an *ilarch*, a *tetrarch* and a senior trooper respectively. It is known that Alexander gave gold crowns to his troops as an award for bravery, however, so this could be an alternative, though less likely, explanation for the wreaths (one of which is silver). The figure on the sarcophagus with a wreathed helmet also wears bracelets. These are certainly badges of rank, as gold bracelets and chains were used as insignia of rank by the Persians.

The long cavalry spear (*xyston*), though made of strong cornel wood, frequently shattered in action, so it was fitted with a second spearhead at the butt end to enable the trooper to continue fighting if this should happen. The *xyston* was not couched under the arm like a knight's lance, but was used to stab at the unprotected faces of the enemy horse and rider. The Persian cavalry, using a pair of shorter spears as javelins and fighting-spears, found themselves at a considerable disadvantage against *xysta*. The sword, a secondary weapon, was slung under the left arm, so it is frequently obscured by the cloak in surviving representations. We may guess that it was used principally as a stabbing weapon too, as the cavalry used straight swords in place of the curved sabres (*kopides*) we might have expected. The aristocratic troopers may have preferred to use their own highly decorated swords, with gold embellishment and bone or ivory hilts, similar to those shown on the Alexander mosaic or those recently excavated from Philip's tomb. Greek cavalry did not use shields at this time, though it was normal for generals to be accompanied by their personal shield-bearers to enable them to fight on foot if necessary. In one incident during the Balkan campaigns Alexander orders the Personal Companions and Bodyguards to take up their shields and gallop up a hill, and on reaching the top half of them dismount to fight on foot.

Some cavalrymen wear only a short-sleeved tunic, but most wear a long-sleeved outer tunic over the first. Only the heavy cavalry regiments (Companion, Thessalian, and Allied) were issued with the cuirass. During the early campaigns, either

The Macedonian cloak; in the form of a rolled-out truncated cone, its two inner corners were pinned together. It can be recognised when worn by the single corner hanging both in front of and behind the figure, and by the straight bottom edge. Headdress would be either the beret-like Macedonian *kausia* or a smaller version of the Thessalian sun-hat.

because of the heat or from bravado, Alexander rarely wore a cuirass and this idiosyncracy may have been widely aped by the young noblemen in the heavy cavalry regiments, especially in the Companion Cavalry. Cavalry boots seem to have been standard throughout the cavalry; their pattern is clearly shown on bronzes of Alexander. A soft leather lining 'sock' is held in place by a strap-work over-boot with a sole and heel.

Looking at Plate C1 one could guess that the Greek saddle cloth, made of some shaggy felt-like substance, was dyed in the regimental colour and faced in the squadron colour. Thus it might be medium purple for the Companions, dark purple for the Thessalians, and rose for the *Prodromoi*, faced in green, red, yellow or some other squadron colour—but this is speculative. Over the saddle cloth a pantherskin shabraque is sometimes worn; perhaps they were restricted to officers. The shabraque is formed from the whole animal's pelt—paws, tail, mask and all. The pelt is slit down the spine from the back of the mask to the middle to enable it to be fitted over the horse's head. The neck hole is lined with material, again possibly in the squadron colour. Identical pantherskin shabraques are also shown in contemporary reliefs from Athens and Serrai in Macedonia. Persian saddle cloths are sometimes used. These probably do not represent booty, as highly decorated Persian saddle cloths were much favoured by the aristocracy and had long been a luxury import into the Greek world. The cuirass-girdle may also have been in the squadron colour.

Companion Cavalry

The Companion (*hetairoi*) Cavalry, the senior regiment of the army, was recruited from the noble youth of Macedonia. Diodorus gives the regiment's strength at the start of the expedition as 1,800, but perhaps some squadrons were left in Macedonia. The regiment was divided into eight squadrons, the first being the Royal Squadron (*basilikē ilē*), which was the vanguard (*agēma*) squadron of the regiment and held the position of honour in the battle line. The Royal Squadron, in whose ranks the Personal Companions fought, was maintained at double strength. The other seven squadrons, at the normal strength of 200 lances each, formed up on the left of the Royal Squadron according to the order of

This small marble head, broken from a battle relief, probably represents Alexander. The neck is tilted slightly to the left, the eyes uplifted and the mouth slightly open—all personal idiosyncracies of Alexander which were so well known as to be copied by his successors, in much the same way as Napoleon's contemporaries aped his habit of putting one hand inside his coat. (Metropolitan Museum of Art, New York)

precedence for the day. The line squadrons are generally named after their commanders in the texts, but each was recruited from a different area of Macedonia and their official designations were probably territorial. In Asia we hear of the squadrons of Bottiaea, Amphipolis, Apollonia, Anthemus, and the so-called 'Leugaean' squadron, and an Upper Macedonian squadron is mentioned during the Balkan Campaigns. The other squadron names are lost.

Two horsemen on the Alexander Sarcophagus can be identified as Companion Cavalrymen. They both wear long-sleeved tunics of medium purple and golden-yellow cloaks with medium purple borders. The cloak (*chlamys*) is of the Macedonian type, so they must be Macedonians, and the colours suggest an élite unit. Furthermore Diodorus (17.77.5) tells us that following the death of Darius Alexander distributed Persian cloaks with purple borders to the Companions. The same colour combination reappears in Hellenistic representations which may also be of Companions (see

21

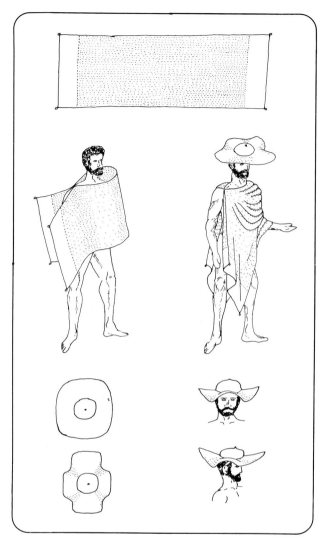

The Thessalian cloak; oblong in shape, it was pinned together along the top edge some distance from the corners, which were allowed to fall. It can be recognised by the two corners falling both in front of and behind the figure, and from its very uneven edge. Headdress would be the wide-brimmed Thessalian sun-hat.

The cuirass was made of small metal plates, linked together, lined or covered with leather or linen, in this case white, which made the cuirass resilient but at the same time more flexible. The length of Alexander's *xyston* has probably been exaggerated on the mosaic to fit the figures into the composition better.

Thessalian Cavalry

Our sources frequently state that the Thessalians were the best cavalry unit in the whole army. This is not surprising as they were raised from the aristocracy of Thessaly, the finest horsemen in the Greek world. For political and social reasons, however, the Companions were the senior regiment in the army and fought under Alexander's direct command, and the Thessalians were usually relegated to a position of lesser importance on the left wing.

Diodorus gives the Thessalians a strength of 1,800 on the crossing into Asia. This figure is the same as that given for the Companion Cavalry, and we may assume that the Thessalian regiment was organised in the same way too, that is divided into eight *ilai*. Their vanguard squadron was the Pharsalian *ilē*, the 'finest and most numerous' squadron (Arrian 3.11.10), which formed Parmenio's personal body-guard on the left wing at Gaugamela. It was the Thessalian regiment's counterpart to the Royal squadron of the Companions, and we may assume that it too was a double-strength squadron of 400. The names of the other seven *ilai* are not given by the historians, but it is fairly certain that they would have been named after the other principal cities of Thessaly in which they had been raised (such as Larisa, Pherae, Tricca, Pharcadon, Pelinna, Oloo-son and Philippi/Philippopolis—ancient Gomphi). Two hundred Thessalian horse joined the army at Gordium, but these were probably used to make up losses in the existing squadrons, rather than to create a ninth *ilē*.

The Thessalian regiment was disbanded at Ecbatana, when the allied contingents were sent back to Greece, but 130 volunteers stayed with the army. These Thessalian volunteers were formed into their own small unit, 'but even this little squadron soon wearied of endless hardship in the pursuit of Bessus, and after less than a year of mercenary service under the former hipparch

Head, p. 104).

On the Pompeiian mosaic Alexander appears wearing the uniform of an officer of Companion Cavalry. He is shown bare-headed for artistic reasons, but a small marble head broken from a battle-relief shows him wearing the standard Boeotian helmet of the cavalry. He also wears a purple cloak with golden-yellow border, the badge of a Personal Companion or Friend, in place of the standard regimental colours. We may presume, by comparison with Plate C2, that the rest of the regiment also normally wore a white cuirass of similar type with a girdle in the squadron colour.

Another Roman gold medallion from Tarsus shows Alexander out hunting. A short hunting spear has replaced the *xyston*, but otherwise the details of Alexander's dress and equipment concur with our other evidence. Note the pantherskin shabraque. The curve of the lower edge of the cuirass over the abdomen is probably an anachronism. (Bibliothèque Nationale, Paris)

Philippus, it was finally disbanded before the Oxus was crossed.' (H. D. Westlake, *Thessaly in the Fourth Century* BC, p. 227–8).

Two horsemen on the Alexander Sarcophagus, one at the hunt and one in battle, wear the distinctive Thessalian cloak—the national dress of Thessaly, identifiable by the two points hanging down both in front and behind the figure. These cloak-ends used to billow out behind the galloping horseman and gave the cloak its Greek nickname of 'Thessalian wings'. The two horsemen are certainly members of the Thessalian cavalry. These cloaks are a very dark purple in colour, with a white border at each end. Both men wear a short-sleeved red under-tunic, but only the fighting Thessalian wears a purple long-sleeved tunic on top. Otherwise the details of dress are similar to the Companions, or general for the whole cavalry; the white cuirass, similar to that worn by Alexander on the Issus mosaic, should be noted.

The Allied Horse

The Greek states of the Corinthian League were obliged to make contributions both of cavalry and of infantry to the expeditionary force. Clearly, not all these states were asked to furnish cavalry.

Diodorus tells us that 600 Greek horse under the command of Erigyius crossed to Asia with the army. These are probably the three squadrons mentioned as fighting under Erigyius at Gaugamela; the squadron of Peloponnesian and Achaean horse, the cavalry of Phthiotis and Malis, and the squadron of Locrian and Phocian horse. At the Granicus the allied cavalry were commanded by Philip son of Menelaus; this is presumably a temporary command, but we are not told why Erigyius was absent from the battle. Reinforcements which reached the army at Gordium included a further 150 horsemen from Elis. 'The Peloponnesian and other allied cavalry' fight with Parmenio on the left wing at Issus, but their commander is not given.

No Greek city seems to have made an individual contribution of a full squadron; rather, each squadron seems to be formed by brigading together the various contingents from a particular area. Our sources do not give us a complete picture of all the reinforcements reaching the army in Asia; information concerning the expansion of the army before the Gaugamela campaign is particularly lacking. We know that Alexander did not take all the army into Egypt, but left a portion of it in Syria. Whilst the ancient authors dwell at length on Alexander's activities in Egypt and mention the reinforcements reaching him there, we know virtually nothing about what had been happening to the rest of the army. The allied cavalry had been detached to the satrap of Syria after the battle of Issus, and it probably received further reinforcements while stationed there. Even before Issus, Curtius reports a speech delivered to Darius by the Greek soldier of fortune Charidemus which mentions 'the Thessalian horse and the Acarnanians and Aetolians', so it is possible that an Acarnanian and Aetolian squadron had already reached the army; but this speech may just be rhetoric invented by Curtius and put into the mouth of Charidemus to enliven his account. We are certain, though, that a Boeotian squadron reached the army in Asia, for an inscription found at Orchomenus records a dedication made by men who had served with Alexander in Asia and mentions their *ilarch*.

At Gaugamela, then, we hear of one brigade of Allied Horse (*hoi xymmachoi hippeis*) commanded by Erigyius son of Larichus, consisting of the squadron

The bronze Boeotian helmets worn by the cavalry were made by hammering out sheet bronze on an armourer's workshop model. This interesting example of such a model, carved from limestone, was found in Memphis; it is possibly of a later date. (Allard Pierson Museum, Amsterdam)

of Peloponnesians and Achaeans, the squadron of Phthiotis and Malis, and the squadron of Locris and Phocis. I presume these are the 600 who crossed into Asia with Erigyius. On the opposite (left) wing, however, we hear of a second brigade of Allied Horse commanded by Coeranus. I would guess that the second brigade also numbered 600 and was divided into three squadrons, probably including a squadron of Boeotians, and possibly including a squadron of Acarnanians and Aetolians. The Eleians could have either fought in the Peloponnesian and Achaean squadron on the right or in a third squadron on the left. The regiment of Allied Horse was disbanded at Ecbatana, but many men enrolled into the Mercenary Horse.

From their position in the various battles we can probably assume that the Allied Horse were a unit of heavy cavalry. Unfortunately no details of their dress or equipment have survived (but see Plates E2, E3).

The Prodromoi

Prodromoi or 'scouts' is a name usually applied only to the four squadrons of Thracian light cavalry belonging to the Royal Army, but occasionally to the other squadrons of Thracian auxiliary cavalry serving with the army too. The *prodromoi* of the Royal Army were probably recruited from inside the borders of Macedonia, from the Thracian provinces annexed by Philip, and served under Macedonian officers. The light cavalry squadrons seem to have been somewhat under strength at the crossing of the Hellespont, for Diodorus tells us that the *prodromoi* and the Paeonian squadron only numbered 900. Presumably the *prodromoi*, the Paeonian squadron and the Odrysian cavalry were brought fully up to strength by the reinforcement of 500 Thracian cavalry which reached the army at Memphis. A further reinforcement of 600 joined the army in Sittacene.

The Thracian cavalry were a wild, uncivilised group of soldiery, who would compare well to the Croats of the Thirty Years' War. They were much given to drink, women and booty. These habits seem to have been adopted by the Macedonian officers set over them. When King Alexander gave over the city of Thebes for plunder, one Alexander, the Macedonian commander of an *ilē* of Thracians but 'in no way like his namesake', broke into the house of a noblewoman called Timocleia. 'Without showing the least respect for the ancestry or the estate of the woman' he drank the cellar dry, had his pleasure of Timocleia, and then forced her to show him where the family gold was hidden. She told him it was hidden at the bottom of a well in the garden; and the avaricious *ilarch* would not wait till morning to inspect the loot, but climbed down the well immediately, dressed only in his tunic. Timocleia promptly repaid his bad manners by rolling boulders down the well and burying him alive. On hearing of the incident the king spared Timocleia and her family on account of her bravery.

The primary role of the *prodromoi*, as the name indicates, was to scout ahead of the advancing army. For this purpose they were occasionally brigaded with units of light infantry or detachments of heavy cavalry. During the Balkan campaigns some units of cavalry used javelins; these are probably *prodromoi*, who seem to have been equipped with the *xyston* and javelins in the first years of Alexander's reign. After the crossing of the Hellespont, however, the terms *prodromoi* and *sarissophoroi* are used indiscriminately and javelins are never mentioned again, so it seems that Alexander re-equipped them with the infantry pike before the expedition crossed over.

As far as defensive armament is concerned, we know from scattered references that the *prodromoi* did use helmets, but probably no other body-armour. A wall-painting in a chamber tomb, known as the 'Kinch' tomb from the name of its Danish excavator, provides us with some uniform details for the light cavalry. The tomb was discovered near Naoussa in Central Macedonia, some distance from the Thracian provinces in which the *prodromoi* were recruited. This is no obstacle to our identification, however, as the unit was commanded by senior officers drawn from the Macedonian nobility. The horseman is shown bearded, so the relief must date to Philip's reign, not Alexander's; he is spearing a Persian infantryman with his *xyston*. It is logical to assume that the horseman died fighting as a member of the advanced force Philip sent into Asia in the spring of 336. Duncan Head (p. 105) has also identified the painting with the *prodromoi*. Upon Alexander's accession or shortly afterwards the beards would be shaved off, bronze Boeotian helmets would be substituted for the painted 'Phrygian' helmets, and *sarissai* for *xysta*. The horse has the ubiquitous pantherskin shabraque, but it does not seem to be lined in any squadron colour. The regimental colour would seem to be the rose colour of the cloak and the trunk of the tunic, but it is not possible to guess which of the other colours might have been a squadron colour.

Thracian Cavalry

The four squadrons of the Royal Army were supplemented by further squadrons of auxiliary Thracian cavalry. The Paeonian squadron crossed the Hellespont with the army. The Paeonians seem to be a detachment of cavalry contributed to the expedition by the client king of Paeonia, for they are commanded by a prince of the Paeonian royal house called Ariston. The Odrysian cavalry were probably contributed in a similar way by the king of the Odrysians, but they were under the command of a Macedonian, Agathon son of Tyrimmas. The Odrysians joined the expedition in time to take part in the battle of Granicus. They were probably two squadrons strong at Gaugamela.

While we may assume that the Paeonian and Odrysian squadrons were equipped in a similar fashion to the regular squadrons of *prodromoi*, their general appearance and dress could have been markedly different as they were not part of the Royal Army. A Paeonian coin shows a warrior,

This bronze Boeotian helmet was found in June 1854 in the bed of the Tigris River at the confluence with its tributary the Sert (the ancient 'Centrites') near Tille in present-day Turkey. Mr R. B. Oakley of Oswaldkirk, Yorkshire, was travelling down the Tigris to Mosul by raft. One of the boatmen pushed his boathook into the stream to keep the raft from running ashore, and when he lifted it out of the water this helmet was caught on the hook! It was bought for the equivalent of about one shilling, and brought to Britain; at one time donated to Rugby School, it is now in the Ashmolean Museum, Oxford. (Ashmolean Museum)

dressed in a long-sleeved tunic, wearing a crested 'Attic' helmet, and equipped with a spear, riding a horse with a pantherskin saddle cloth. He spears a warrior on foot who is shown wearing trousers. Coins of this series have been identified with an incident in the Gaugamela campaign when Ariston, the commander of the Paeonian squadron, speared Satropates through the throat. The identification, however, is still far from certain.

Alexander was in process of crossing the Tigris; the infantry were wading across with considerable difficulty, but the king, together with a small advance party of light cavalry, had reached the far bank. Suddenly a flying column of 1,000 Persian cavalry commanded by Satropates appeared to dispute the crossing. The situation was critical— only the advance party was formed up on the river bank and the unformed infantry, struggling in the water with their packs, would fall easy prey to a quick charge. Alexander immediately ordered forward the Paeonian squadron, with Ariston at its head. From the river the whole army watched the drama unfolding on the steep riverbank.

Ariston made straight for the Persian colonel, Satropates, and promptly ran him through the throat with his spear. The Persian turned and tried to make his way back to safety among his comrades.

A broken relief in Bursa Museum, Turkey, found recently in the vicinity of that town. The lower part of this interesting sculpture shows heavy cavalry attacking Greek(?) infantry. Note the Boeotian helmets, the cuirasses, and the Greek and Persian saddle cloths. The piece must date to the reign of Alexander or shortly thereafter. (German Archaeological Institute, Istanbul)

Ariston overtook his victim, unhorsed him, and, after a brief but desperate struggle, severed his head with a sword-cut. The Paeonian prince gathered up Satropates' head and galloped back to the King, to the accompaniment of wild cheering from the army. Throwing his trophy at Alexander's feet the Paeonian shouted, 'Among us, oh King, such a present is rewarded with a golden drinking-horn!' 'An empty one, I suppose,' replied Alexander with a laugh, 'but I promise you one full of untempered wine.'

The Mercenary Cavalry
Alexander was deficient in light cavalry in his early campaigns. The mercenary cavalry were raised to offset this deficiency, a serious one, particularly in the Gaugamela campaign, where Alexander's strategic planning relied heavily on precise information as to the whereabouts of the enemy. We hear of a squadron of 200 mercenary cavalry as early as the siege of Halicarnassus, but these troops were left in Caria as part of the provincial army.

At Gaugamela we hear of two brigades of mercenary horse, the 'Foreign Mercenary Cavalry' under Andromachus son of Hieron and the 'Mercenary Cavalry' under Menidas. It is usually assumed that the latter unit is to be identified with the 400 Greek mercenaries who joined the expedition at Memphis under the command of 'Menoitas son of Hegesander'. The 'Foreign Mercenary Cavalry' were presumably of the same strength, two squadrons, but we are not told whether they had been raised earlier or at the same time as Menidas' unit, possibly in Syria.

Alexander seems to have considered these new, and as yet untried regiments to have been expendable. At Gaugamela Andromachus' unit is stationed in front of the left wing, while Menidas rides point to the whole army on the right wing. Battle commenced when Alexander ordered Menidas to charge the Scythian and Bactrian brigades of armoured cavalry, the latter unit alone some thousand sabres strong. The mercenary cavalry certainly earned their pay on 30 September 331 BC, and Menidas himself all but died of multiple arrow wounds received later on in the battle.

When the Greek allies were dismissed at Ecbatana, Alexander encouraged all who wished to continue to serve in the army to enrol as mercenaries, and we are told that many did so. The mercenary cavalry was expanded with those of the Allied Horse who signed on, supplemented with newly recruited mercenaries sent east, and the new units were commanded by officers previously serving in the Allied Horse. The precise details are obscure, and the evidence is open to various interpretations, but the picture *seems* to be as follows.

Both Menidas and Andromachus together with their troops were left behind under Parmenio in Media when Alexander pushed on to hunt down Darius. Soon after we hear that command of the 'Mercenary Cavalry' had passed to Philip son of Menelaus, who had commanded the Allied Horse at the Granicus. Andromachus retained command of the 'Foreign Mercenary Cavalry'. Meanwhile we hear that Alexander has taken the Mercenary Cavalry under Erigyius with him. In the middle of 330, therefore, there are at least three units of mercenary horse.

One year later, during operations near Samarkand, Alexander hears that the garrison left behind in that city was being besieged by Spitamenes. He sends back a relief column consisting of about 60 Companions, 800 mercenary horse, and a detachment of mercenary infantry, retaining one *hipparchy* of mercenary horse under his command. The whole of the relief column, worn out by a long forced march, was ambushed by Scythian horse-archers and exterminated while trying to withdraw towards the River Polytimetus. Only 40 cavalry and about 300 infantry escaped.

The relief column was rather ineffectually commanded by Pharnuches, and under him are mentioned Menedemus, who presumably commanded the infantry, as well as Andromachus and Caranus, each, presumably, commanding 400 cavalry. During the account of the fighting Caranus, who may possibly be identified with the Coeranus who commanded the second brigade of Allied Horse at Gaugamela, is called a *hipparch*, but there is no indication anywhere that he holds any authority over Andromachus. It seems wisest to conclude that there continued to be three units of mercenary horse, each two *ilai* strong, each now called a *hipparchy*. Caranus may have taken over command of one of these units from Erigyius or Philip, but it is just possible that there were four hipparchies, the fourth having escaped from our texts.

The description of the unequal fight between Menidas' cavalry and the Bactrians at Gaugamela makes it obvious that the mercenary horse were but lightly equipped. Probably they fought with spear and swords and wore only the Boeotian helmet, boots, tunic and cloak. No representation survives which can be associated with the regiment, but their appearance was probably identical to that of the *prodromoi*, only the colours being different.

The Infantry

Organisation and Tactics

At the lowest level the tactical unit of the infantry was the *dekas* which, as the name implies, had once consisted of ten men, expanded to 16 well before Alexander's reign. The *dekas* formed one file of the phalanx.

Normally the files would be drawn up in close order (*pyknos*, *pyknōsis*), 16 deep with each man occupying a yard square. Locked shields (*synaspismos*) was a formation usually only adopted when receiving rather than delivering a charge. It was achieved by inserting the rear half of each file into the spaces between the front halves of the file. The depth of the phalanx would now be eight yards, with each man occupying a frontage of one cubit (half a yard). Both formations, however, were found to be too cramped for manoeuvring or advancing in an orderly manner, so prior to contact the phalanx would be drawn up in an open order with a depth of two files (32 yards) with each double file occupying a frontage of two yards. This was probably called 'deep order' (*bathos*) in Alexander's army. In all these formations, obviously, the frontage occupied by the phalanx remained constant.

During all these evolutions the spear would not be lowered, as it would obstruct free manoeuvre; the lowering of the spears was only ordered before the charge, which was sometimes carried out at the run if rapid movement were required to exploit the tactical situation. The charge would be delivered to the accompaniment of the Macedonian battle-cry—'Alalalalai!'—offered to Enyalios, a Greek epithet for Ares, the god of war. The prior advance was, in contrast, carried out in perfect silence to give the battle-cry maximum psychological effect.

The army usually marched in column, it seems, with the phalanx split into two wings. The exact manner in which the phalanx would deploy from column into line is not, as yet, fully understood, but the advance of the phalanx in ever closer formation is nicely described in an account of the battle of Issus written by the contemporary historian Callisthenes (and contained in Polybius 12.19.6):

> 'Immediately on issuing into the open country he re-formed his order, passing to all the word of command to form into phalanx, making it at first 32 deep, changing this subsequently to 16 deep, and finally as he approached the enemy to 8 deep.'

Alexander, at the end of his life, intended to incorporate Persian archers and javelinmen into the phalanx, and Arrian's account of the proposed change (7.23.3–4) mentions that the file was commanded by a *dekadarch*, and contained a *dimoirites* and two *dekastateroi* or 'ten-stater men'.

27

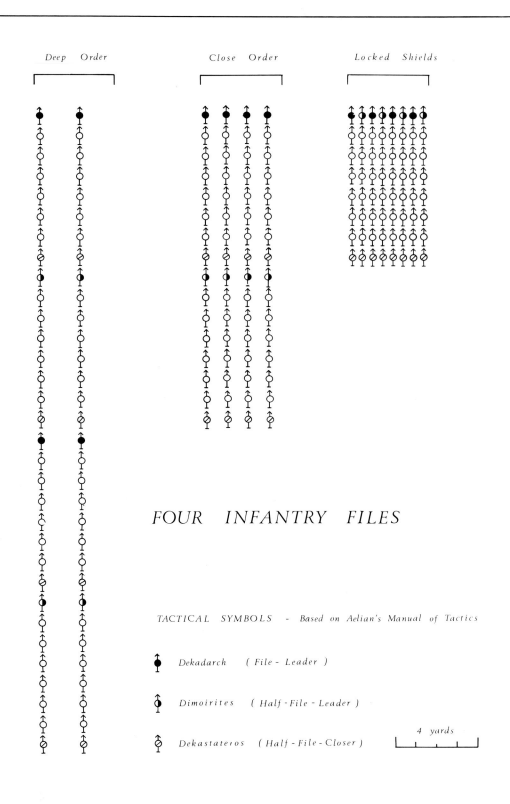

Deep Order *Close Order* *Locked Shields*

FOUR INFANTRY FILES

TACTICAL SYMBOLS - *Based on Aelian's Manual of Tactics*

Dekadarch   (*File - Leader*)

Dimoirites   (*Half - File - Leader*)

Dekastateros   (*Half - File - Closer*)

4 yards

28

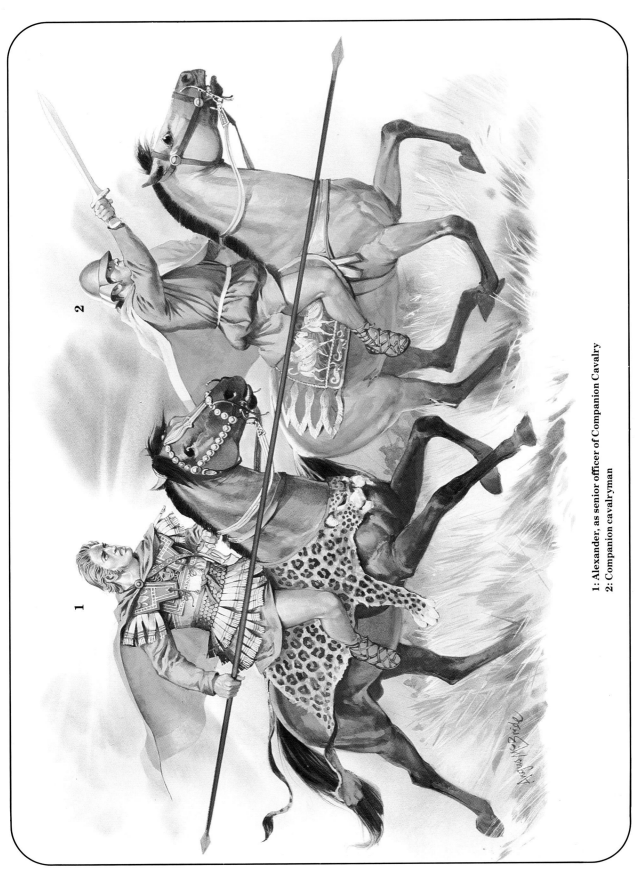

1: Alexander, as senior officer of Companion Cavalry
2: Companion cavalryman

A

1: Companion cavalryman, hunting dress
2: Royal Page, hunting dress
3: Personal Companion, hunting dress

B

1: Thessalian cavalryman, hunting dress
2: Officer, Thessalian Cavalry

1

2

C

1: Cavalryman of the 'Prodromoi'
2: Infantryman, camp dress
3: Foot Companion, hunting dress

D

1: Hypaspist
2, 3 : Soldiers of unidentified unit

E

1: Foot Companion
2: Greek mercenary in Persian service
3: Officer of Foot Companions

F

1: Senior soldier of Foot Companions
2: Foot Companion
3: Servant

G

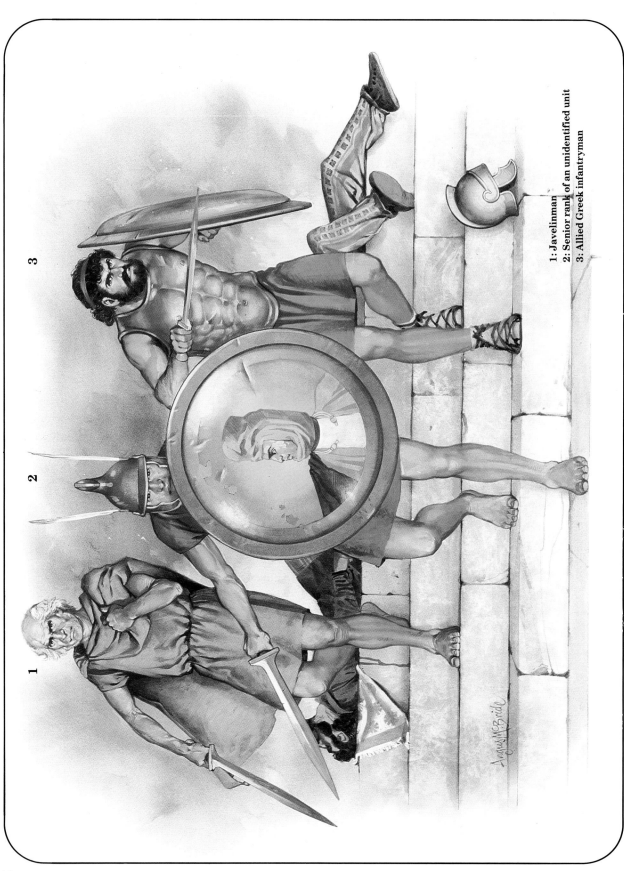

1: Javelinman
2: Senior rank of an unidentified unit
3: Allied Greek infantryman

H

Coin of King Antimachos II of Bactria. Only fragments remain of the history of the Greeks and Macedonians in the East after the time of Alexander; we know that they conquered the Punjab, and many embraced Buddhism. They were eventually overrun by steppe tribes from the north. Antimachos is shown wearing the beret-like *kausia*, **national headdress of Macedonia, and the royal diadem; Alexander is mentioned as wearing the same combination on occasion.**

Dimoirites literally means something like 'two-part man' and is usually translated as 'double-pay man', which is its sense in Xenophon. In Hellenistic times, however, the 16-man file was divided into four quarters, and the half-file is called a *dimoiria* and is commanded by a *dimoirites* (Asclepiodotus 2.2), so this is probably a better interpretation. Originally, then, it seems that the *dekadarch* commanded the file and the first half-file, and the *dimoirites*, standing in the ninth rank of the file, led the second half-file. The two *dekastateroi* probably brought up the rear of each half-file and stood in the eighth and 16th ranks. These senior soldiers were the equivalent of our junior NCOs.

An infantry company (*lochos*) would consist of 512 men drawn up in 32 files and so would occupy a frontage of 32 yards. It was the basic administrative and organisational unit of the infantry and we hear of no sub-divisions. The *lochos* was commanded by an officer called a *lochagos*. Later on in Alexander's reign the company is sometimes called a 'five-hundred' and its commander a *pentekosiarch* or 'commander of five-hundred'. We may also assume that each company also had a *hypēretes* and a trumpeter to pass on orders. A number of companies, usually two or three, would comprise a battalion or *taxis*. In some regiments the battalion was called a 'thousand' or *chiliarchy*, but this term was never used if the battalion had more than two *lochoi*.

On the march

Each *dekas* was allowed one servant to look after its heavy baggage, which was carried by a baggage animal, usually a mule or donkey. When the army reached Egypt, and afterwards, an increasing use was made of camels, who were able to carry more and who were more suitable for campaigning in Asia. The servants were called *ektaktoi*, or supernumeraries, because they did not fight in the ranks.

The bulkiest items the *dekas* had were its tents. We do not know how many men constituted a tent-party, whether a full file, half-file, or quarter-file. The tents were carried in waterproof leather tent-covers which acted as fly-sheets when the tents were erected. During river crossings these tent-covers were sewn together and stuffed with chaff to make floating rafts. Usually the animals would be ferried across on these rafts while the men would cross over supported by inflated water-skins. The water-skins would normally be carried by the baggage animal, as would the iron tent pegs and the guy ropes. We hear of axes being used, and we know that each *dekas* carried a hand-mill: presumably other implements and construction tools were issued down to the level of the *dekas*.

The infantry usually marched with their own weapons and armour, but the uncomfortable helmet was replaced by the *kausia*, a beret-style cap, the regional headdress of Macedonia. A personal pack was also carried. We know this included a bed-roll, for in India the men had to sleep with their bedding slung from the trees to get away from the snakes. It would also include a drinking cup and other domestic items. The men also carried their own food, which would be ready-cooked if rapid movement were required. Cooking was extremely slow and difficult in the days before flint and steel came into use during the Middle Ages. It was normal Greek military practice to carry fire in some form or other inside earthenware pots.

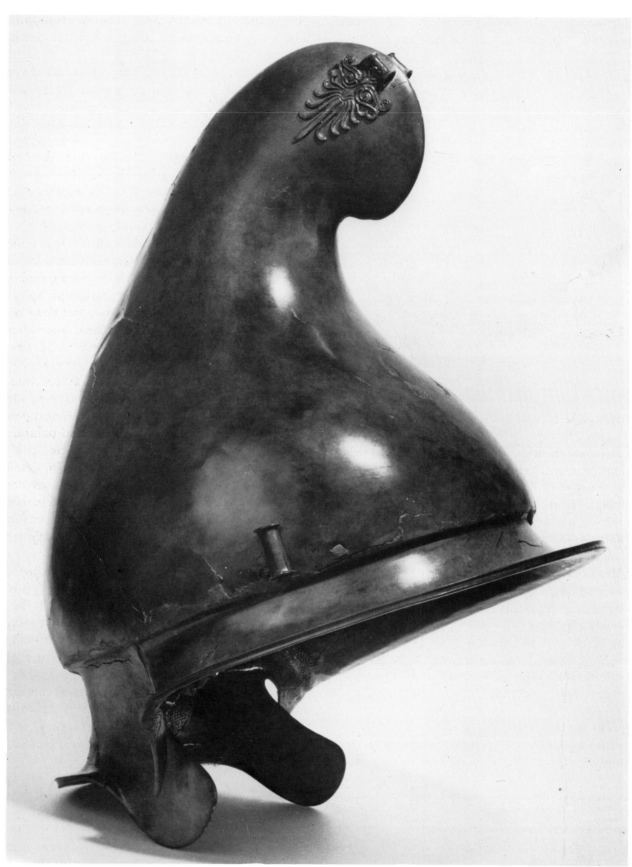

38

These may have been carried by the servants, possibly with some dry kindling.

The other personal possessions of the soldiery were carried in the baggage wagons, as was their booty. The sick also travelled in wagons, possibly in special ambulances. The baggage train consisted of these wagons and others containing artillery and siege engines in kit form, accompanied by the families of the soldiers and the sutlers following the army, marching at the back of the army protected by a rearguard.

An interesting passage in Curtius (6.2.16) describes the scene in camp when the army is gripped by a rumour that the king is about to return to Macedonia:

> 'They ran as though crazed to their tents and made ready their packs for the journey; you would believe that the signal to march had been given throughout the whole camp. Here the noise of those looking for their tent-mates, there of those loading the wagons, was borne to the king's ears.'

Infantry Equipment

The infantrymen on the Alexander Sarcophagus all use hoplite shields. Most modern authorities believe that the infantry under Alexander continued to use the *peltai* they had used during the first years of Philip's reign, but this view runs against the archaeological evidence, and against some evidence contained in the texts. In one battle during the Balkan campaigns Arrian (1.1.9) tells us that the Thracians intended to launch carts down a hillside to break up the advancing phalanx. Alexander ordered the phalanx to crouch down and link their shields closely together. The carts slid over the shields and not one man perished. It is difficult to see how this operation could have been successfully performed without large shields. Curtius mentions similar 'tortoise' tactics being used during the campaign against the Uxians and the storming of the Persian Gates.

Many infantrymen on the Sarcophagus also wear cuirasses, but again most modern authorities do not

An interesting helmet of the 'Phrygian' type, recently excavated and published by Mrs J. Votokopolou, the Ephor of Ioannina Museum, who has kindly supplied the photograph. Though possibly a little later than Alexander's reign, it is useful in that the tubular plume-holders fixed to the visor give us some idea of how to reconstruct the plumes attached to the helmets of Alexander's infantry.

believe that the infantry were so heavily equipped. The heavy armour of the phalanx is mentioned in Arrian's description (1.28.7) of the Pisidian campaign, however, and Diodorus (17.44.2) tells us that the Tyrians poured hot sand over their Macedonian besiegers, which passed underneath cuirasses and clothing and brought about a horrible death. Finally Diodorus (17.95.4) mentions that 25,000 infantry panoplies were issued in India, and Curtius (9.3.22) adds that the old sets were burned. It seems, then, that at least some of the infantry used cuirasses, manufactured in part from some combustible material such as linen or leather.

The helmets are of the 'Phrygian' type: some helmets are left plain bronze, but most are painted blue, which may have been the distinguishing colour of the infantry. A few helmets have gilt spines running along the 'cockscomb' crest, and this may be an officer's badge of rank. These and other helmets without the spine have fittings for plumes, which are missing from the Sarcophagus. The plumes have been restored as long feathers, from one helmet painted behind a figure on the Sarcophagus, and from coins showing Alexander. One helmet in a later Macedonian wall-painting shows plumes in the form of horsehair 'tails', however, and restorations incorporating this detail are equally possible. Swords and scabbards are not shown on some of the figures, but it would seem that the artist had deliberately chosen to leave them out, and we can probably assume that all the infantry were issued with swords.

No spears are shown in use on the Sarcophagus. The infantry used a long spear of Balkan origin called the *sarissa*. Theophrastus in his *Historia Plantarum* (3.12.1–2) tells us that the longest [*sic*] *sarissai* measured 12 cubits (18 feet), but he compiled this work after becoming professor at Athens in 322 BC, so this only gives us a maximum length for the spears used by the armies of Alexander's successors. *Sarissai* may have been shorter during Alexander's reign, but even so one presumes that they would have been held underarm with both hands.

Apart from its length the most distinctive feature of the *sarissa* was its small iron head, which made it more suitable for piercing armour than the large-headed Greek hoplite spear. A Roman writer on hunting (Grattius, *Cynegeticon* 117–120) warns us to

avoid the enormous Macedonian pikes with their small 'teeth' as unsuitable for hunting. The *sarissa* seems to have been furnished with a spear-butt, although this is not absolutely certain. A bronze spear-butt in the Greek Museum of the University of Newcastle upon Tyne may provide us with such an example. This object has many interesting features and is well worth describing at some length (see accompanying photo). The spear-butt is cast and is very heavy; inside are traces of the pitch used to fix it to the shaft. During cleaning in 1977 black lettering was discovered at the top underneath the layers of corrosion. Between two narrow bands are the letters MAK, an abbreviation for 'Macedonian' and an indication that the piece was issued by the state. One is reminded of the 'WD broad arrow' used to this day to mark British Army property. Similar black-painted bands can be observed on some of the iron pike heads on the Pompeiian mosaic. A date in the later 4th century BC has been suggested for the spear-butt, but certainty is impossible.

The Foot Companions

The Foot Companions (*pezhetairoi*) numbered 9,000, divided into six battalions (*taxeis*) of three *lochoi* each. The *taxeis* were normally named after their commanders. Four *taxeis* had the same commanders down to 330 BC: those of Coenus son of Polemocrates, Perdiccas son of Orontes, Craterus son of Alexander, and Meleager son of Neoptolemus. The *taxis* of Amyntas son of Andromenes was temporarily commanded by his brother Simmias while Amyntas was back in Macedonia levying reinforcements. The last *taxis* was commanded by Philip son of Amyntas at Granicus, by Ptolemaios son of Seleucus at Issus, at which battle he was killed, and afterwards by Polyperchon son of Simmias. The battalions would be drawn up on the battlefield in order of precedence for the day, although Coenus' *taxis*, which seems to be of élite status, occupies the position of honour on the right wing at Issus and Gaugamela. Some of the *taxeis*, including Coenus', were termed *asthetairoi*, which could be a term for élite battalions or for battalions recruited in Upper Macedonia.

Bronze spear-butt: the lettering appeared during cleaning in 1977. (Greek Museum, University of Newcastle upon Tyne)

Detail of the Alexander Mosaic from Pompeii showing a stand of Macedonian pikes foreshadowing the doom of the Persian King Darius. Note the painted bands around the spear sockets. (German Archaeological Institute, Rome)

Each *taxis* was raised from a different district of Macedonia, from which it probably took its official designation. Unfortunately the 'ethnics' of the *taxeis* of the Foot Companions are only given in the descriptions of Alexander's forces at Gaugamela contained in Diodorus and Curtius, which, although based on a common source, differ from each other. Both are garbled and both differ from Arrian. The problem is still the subject of considerable scholarly debate, but one possible interpretation is that Coenus' *taxis* is Elymiotid, Perdiccas' is Orestid, Meleager's is Lyncestian, and Polyperchon's is Tymphiot. So it is possible that at least half of the six *taxeis* were recruited from the separatist cantons of Upper Macedonia; perhaps all were. This could be deliberate policy on Alexander's part, leaving only the more politically reliable battalions recruited from the heart of the kingdom back in Macedonia with Antipater.

Only five phalangites are shown clothed on the Alexander Sarcophagus, and of these four wear cuirasses. These figures certainly represent Foot Companions. No two figures are dressed and equipped alike, so one must assume that they represent four separate *taxeis*. No figure can be associated with a particular *taxis* with any certainty, but one of the four, clad in a purple tunic, may belong to an élite battalion—possibly *asthetairoi*, perhaps Coenus' Elymiotid battalion. The bronze shields have a coloured medallion painted in their centre. These seem to show the heads of deities, perhaps ones with local associations: probably each battalion had its own shield-device.

The Hypaspists

Hypaspistes means 'shield-bearer' in Greek. The official name of the regiment seems to have been 'The Hypaspists of the Companions' (*hoi hypaspistoi*

Detail of the Alexander Mosaic from Pompeii. This infantryman, wearing a purple *kausia* and a red cloak, is possibly an officer of Hypaspists. (German Archaeological Institute, Rome)

(*agēma*) were known as 'The Royal (*basilikoi*) Hypaspists', and were composed of men selected out of the whole army for their height. This *lochos* (possibly expanded to a *chiliarchy* later) guarded the king's tent in camp and always took the place of honour in the battle-line, the other companies forming up on the left in order of precedence for the day.

The Hypaspists acted as a flexible link between the Companion Cavalry and the Foot Companions. When the cavalry advanced the Hypaspists had to be able to move forward rapidly in order to keep up with them. It is logical to assume that they were more lightly equipped than the Foot Companions. In several places the texts talk of Alexander taking the lightest armed of the phalanx (or of the hoplites) with him, and we should assume that the Hypaspists are meant. Whenever Alexander detaches a 'flying column' from the army the Hypaspists always form part of it, as they would have been able to keep up with the pace much more easily than the heavily clad Foot Companions.

Of the five clothed hoplites on the Alexander Sarcophagus, one alone does not wear a cuirass, and we should identify this figure as a hypaspist. He is, in fact, wearing the dress and equipment of a Greek hoplite prior to Philip's re-armament. The tunic, let down at the shoulder to allow free movement of the right arm, was known as an *exōmis*. Alone of the infantry the hypaspist wears boots. During the long chases after Darius and Bessus the hypaspists are sometimes mounted two-a-back behind the cavalrymen on their horses, so perhaps boots were worn for such eventualities. In one of the descriptions of the murder of Cleitus, Arrian tells us that some sources say Alexander snatched a spear from a Bodyguard, others say it was a *sarissa* from one of the guards (presumably a hypaspist). A short broken spear is painted on the sarcophagus, together with a shield, lying next to the hypaspist. The spear may belong to him. Also lying next to him is a 'Phrygian' helmet, painted purple with a gilt spine, which could belong to an officer of hypaspists (see Plate E). Vestiges of the figure of a footsoldier, running alongside Alexander on the Pompeiian mosaic and wearing a purple *kausia* and a red (Macedonian?) cloak, may also show an officer of the hypaspists, as we would expect this corps to be shown alongside the cavalry.

tōn hetairōn), and it is generally thought that the regiment had originally been formed from the personal retainers of the king's Companions. This role was continued in a vestigial manner, for the leading hypaspists carried the king's personal weapons, including the Sacred Shield of Troy, before him in battle. The regiment seems to have been 3,000 strong at first, divided into six *lochoi*, and was commanded by Nicanor son of Parmenio until his death in 330. We hear of a number of hypaspist officers in the texts: Admetus (possibly commander of the *agēma*), who dies at Tyre, Philotas, Hellanicus, Adaeus, who dies at Halicarnassus, and Timander. Adaeus is called a *chiliarch*, but this could be an anachronism.

The men of the vanguard *lochos* of the regiment

The Later Army

After Gaugamela the army took Babylon, then marched on Susa. On the road to Susa, passing through the fertile province of Sittacene, it was met by a large reinforcement from Macedonia under the command of Amyntas and consisting of 6,000 Macedonian foot, 600 Macedonian cavalry, 600 Thracian cavalry, 3,500 Trallians, and mercenaries to the number of 4,000 foot and 380 horse. Alexander halted the army and carried out the first of a series of thoroughgoing army re-organisations. He also took the opportunity to introduce some purely administrative reforms, and to promote officers of ability to the vacancies created.

The large number of reinforcements, even after replacing losses and releasing men from service, allowed Alexander to expand the infantry. Curtius seems to be talking of the hypaspists when he tells us that the *lochoi* were grouped into *chiliarchies* which had not existed before(?). New officers were appointed on the basis of military virtue; eight names follow (including Philotas and Hellanicus), so we may presume that the number of *lochoi* was raised to eight. It also seems that a seventh *taxis* was added to the Foot Companions. Next year Alexander leaves 6,000 Macedonian infantry (four *taxeis*) at Ecbatana to guard the treasure, but takes the Hypaspists and the *taxeis* of Coenus, Craterus and Amyntas with him in the pursuit of Darius and the Hyrcanian campaign. Seven *taxeis* are also mentioned at the Hydaspes.

The cavalry was also re-organised. Each *ile* was now divided into two *lochoi* of two troops each, and officers were appointed to command on the basis of ability after a close scrutiny of the military conduct sheets. This reform was probably instituted to ease administrative efficiency, as the *ile* was a rather large force of horses, grooms and riders for one man to administer effectively. Henceforward the cavalry was administered by century (*hekatostuas*), which word becomes interchangeable with *lochos* in the cavalry.

More major changes occurred when the army reached Ecbatana. The Thessalian cavalry and the Allied forces, both cavalry and infantry, were disbanded and sent home. Many, however, remained with the army as mercenaries, and in future much more use is made of mercenaries and Asian troops. Later in his reign Alexander starts to

The Azara herm, now in the Louvre. Found at Tivoli, it was presented to Napoleon by Don José Nicholas de Azara, international diplomat, patron of the arts, man of letters, archaeologist and antiquarian, and representative of the Spanish court first at Rome and later at Paris. The herm shows Alexander at the age of 30—increasingly superstitious, turbulent, and running out of geography. (Louvre, Paris)

levy and train Persian troops, and before his death he planned to integrate these troops into the phalanx.

During the early part of 330 BC, in preparation for the arduous campaigns lying ahead in the mountains and deserts of Iran and Central Asia, the Foot Companions start to lose their armour. A stratagem described in Polyaenus (4.3.13) tells us that Alexander re-equipped his soldiers with the half-cuirass (*hēmithōrakion*) instead of the cuirass, after they had fled, in order that they would not turn their backs on the enemy again. The incident referred to must be Alexander's first (and disastrous) attempt to storm the Persian Gates, and we should accept the information Polyaenus gives us as genuine, even if the reason given for the change is incorrect. During the Hyrcanian campaign Coenus' *taxis* is described as 'the lightest armed of the Macedonian phalanx'; 'the lightest armed of the

This Athenian sepulchral relief, found at Eleusis in 1888, shows the new equipment adopted by the Athenian army after the defeat at Chaeronea: bronze muscle-cuirass with leather groin-flaps, and bronze 'Phrygian' helmet after the Macedonian style. There are many representations of this type in the museums of Athens and Eleusis, all dating to the years 338–317 BC, and many still showing traces of the original colouring. All soldiers seem to wear a red tunic and *ephaptis* and some also wear head-bands. (National Museum, Athens)

It was perhaps when the army entered India that the *sarissai* first reached their enormous length, giving the phalanx greater capability to fight elephants and their drivers. The cuirass had been discarded and normal equipment now consisted of shield, sword, javelin and *sarissa*, held in the left hand at first, then transferred to the right after the javelin had been thrown. At the Hydaspes sabres (*kopides*) are used to attack the trunks of Porus' elephants, and axes to cut off their feet.

The army in India must have presented a strange sight. Before the campaign Alexander had issued the Hypaspists with silvered shields, the cavalry with gilded bits, and the rest of the infantry with gilded and silvered equipment. This sumptuousness was mixed with shabbiness. The lines of supply had started to break down. At first Persian tunics had to be worn, then re-cut Indian ones; cuirasses and other armour wore out and had to be discarded. The morale of the troops had been severely undermined by Porus' elephants, and when a rumour hit the army that an army of 4,000 elephants lay ahead on the other side of the Hyphasis River they mutinied. This fear of elephants was probably the main consideration which induced Alexander to re-distribute armour to the infantry shortly afterwards: the main purpose of armour, after all, is not to protect the wearer, but to make him think he is protected.

Greek Infantry

Some 7,000 Greek allied infantry crossed the Hellespont with Alexander. The corps was composed of contingents sent by the member states of the League of Corinth; each contingent was composed of selected men (*epilektoi*) from the state's army, and served under its own officers. The corps as a whole was commanded by a Macedonian *stratēgos*.

Following the shattering blow delivered to them at Chaeronea, the armies of Greece underwent a series of army reforms aimed at upgrading their equipment so as to enable them to hold their own in the new conditions of general war. In Athens we can see the result of these reforms, carried out in that city under the aegis of the politician Lycurgus, in the gravestones sculpted between 338 and 317 (when ostentatious funerary monuments were banned). Body armour, abandoned since the

phalanx' are mentioned a year later in operations near Maracanda; and in 326 in the advance to the Aornos Rock 'the lightest but at the same time the best [i.e. most suitably] armed' men are selected from *taxeis* other than that of Coenus. So it seems that other *taxeis*, or ranks of other *taxeis*, may have also started to use lighter equipment.

Peloponnesian Wars, is re-introduced in the form of the 'muscle-cuirass', and the Spartan-style *pilos* helmet is replaced by the Macedonian 'Phrygian' helmet. The situation recalls the late 19th century, when the world's armies threw away their shakos and képis and donned spiked helmets. In Megara we do not see the 'Phrygian' helmet appear, but a 'muscle-cuirass' of similar type to the Athenian was adopted. We can assume that similar changes took place in other states in Greece less well known archaeologically. One figure on the Alexander Sarcophagus (Plate H3) can be identified as a Greek, for he has not shaved his beard off, as he would have had to do had he been a member of the Macedonian Army. He also wears a 'muscle-cuirass'.

The army also contained a large number of Greek mercenary infantry. The main role of the mercenary infantry was to provide garrison troops

Originally in the Nani Collection in Venice, this stele was first published by Paciaudi in 1761. It was purchased by the Musée Calvet in 1841 among other marbles from the same collection. The inscription records the award of the office of *proxenos*— 'state representative'—by the state of Athens to the Megarian general Phokinos, who wears the crested helmet of a general and who is followed by two other Megarians. All three wear the muscle-cuirass, but the 'Phrygian' helmet does not appear. (Musée Calvet, Avignon)

to keep newly conquered provinces in check. Troops for this purpose were frequently enrolled on the spot, usually from Greek mercenaries previously in Persian service. These mercenary bands were not altogether reliable; many had anti-Macedonian sympathies, and mutinies were not infrequent, particularly in the later years of Alexander's reign. Mercenaries were also used, however, to supplement the number of infantry in the field army, but these units seem to have been composed of altogether more reliable troops who had been with the army a long time or who had been recruited more recently from friendly states in Greece.

The surviving accounts of the battle of Gaugamela are all individually incomplete and differ significantly from one another, but they seem to mention two separate regiments of mercenaries participating in the battle. The veteran (*archaioi*) mercenaries, who fight on the right wing and are mentioned by Arrian, are probably the 5,000 who originally crossed the Hellespont with Alexander either in part or in full. The Achaean mercenaries, who fight on the left wing and are mentioned by Diodorus and Curtius (though Curtius does not call them Achaean), are probably the 4,000 mercenaries recruited in the Peloponnese which joined the army at Sidon the year before (Arrian 2.20.5).

Greek mercenary infantry at this time were still equipped along traditional Spartan lines, with bronze hoplite shield and helmet but no other body armour, carrying the normal infantry spear and sword, and dressed in red *exōmis* tunics. Certainly Greek mercenary infantry in Persian service appear with this dress and equipment on both the Alexander Sarcophagus (see Plate F2) and the Alexander Mosaic. It is possible that the mercenaries in Macedonian service wore cuirasses, but, given their position on the wings at Gaugamela, where mobility would be crucial, it is more probable that they did not.

Light Infantry

We know precious little of the light infantry (*psiloi*) of the army. They presumably fought in open order, perhaps in less depth than the phalanx, and their sub-units may have occupied greater frontages than those of the phalanx. The basic sub-unit seems to be the company of 500, but we are not sure if these companies were called *lochoi* as they were in the phalanx.

The corps of archers (*toxotai*) as a whole was under the command of a *stratēgos*, and was divided into a number of companies of 500 men, each, it seems, under the command of a *toxarch*. The first *stratēgos*, Cleander, died in the Pisidian campaign and was replaced by Antiochus, who in turn died and was replaced by the Cretan Ombrion in Egypt in 331 BC.

Alexander seems to have had a company of Cretan archers from the beginning of his reign. These Cretans could have been mercenaries, but it is more likely that they were an allied contingent supplied by those cities of Crete favourable to Macedon. They are not mentioned after the dismissal of the allies at Ecbatana. Cretan archers were equipped with a small bronze *peltē*, which

The tomb of Aristonautes, found in Athens in 1864, is well known and widely published. Aristonautes was an officer in the infantry; his dress and equipment are identical to those shown on other Attic tombstones of infantrymen of this period, but his helmet would originally have been circled by an applied metal wreath as the insignia of his rank—the peg-holes for the missing wreath are still visible in the helmet. (National Museum, Athens)

Bronze statuette of Alexander in the Museo Nazionale, Naples. (Anderson)

enabled them to fight at close quarters as well as provide missile fire. The Cretans served under their own officers—Eurybotas, who was killed at Thebes in 335, and thereafter by Ombrion, who was promoted to command of the whole corps of archers at Memphis in 331.

A second company of archers soon joined the expedition under the command of the *toxarch* Clearchus, who died during the siege of Halicarnassus. He seems to have been replaced by Antiochus, who is mentioned as a *toxarch* at Issus, although he doubled as *stratēgos* of the whole corps after the death of Cleander. We do not know the name of the *toxarch* appointed to command the second company after Antiochus' death in 331, nor do we know the nationality of the company, although they may have been Macedonians. A third company, under Briso, joins the expedition before Gaugamela, and these are definitely called Macedonians. The non-Cretans did not, it seems, carry the bronze *peltē*, for Arrian (3.18.5) refers to

'the lightest-armed of the archers' during the storming of the Persian Gates.

The Agrianian javelinmen, under the command of the Macedonian Attalus, were the crack light infantry unit of the army. Plate H1 shows a possible reconstruction of their dress, though *peltai* may have been carried as well as javelins. They were probably supplied for the expedition by the client king of the Agrianians, Langarus, out of his household troops. Only one company was present at the crossing of the Hellespont, but a second company joined the army before Issus, bringing up their strength to 1,000.

Little is known of the other light infantry, who are given the general term of 'Thracians' in the texts. They are the 7,000 Odrysians, Triballians and Illyrians who appear in Diodorus' enumeration of the army which crossed the Hellespont. They could be mercenaries, but given Alexander's shortage of money in the earlier campaigns they are more probably further contingents sent for the expedition by other client kings. Probably all the light infantry were javelinmen (*akontistai*), divided into a number of *taxeis*, although there may also have been some units of slingers. The whole corps may have been under the command of an obscure figure whom Arrian (4.7.2) calls 'Ptolemaios the *stratēgos* of the Thracians'. The Odrysians were

The Alexander Mosaic from Pompeii, a mosaic copy of a masterpiece by a Greek painter contemporary with Alexander. The author of the original work has not yet been identified with any certainty, but leading contenders are Apelles and Philoxenus. (German Archaeological Institute, Rome)

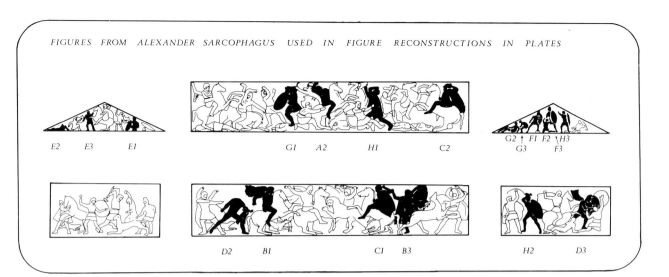

FIGURES FROM ALEXANDER SARCOPHAGUS USED IN FIGURE RECONSTRUCTIONS IN PLATES

commanded by Sitalkes, a prince of the Odrysian royal house, and other units may also have been under native commanders. Another unit of javelinmen was commanded by Balacrus.

The Plates

A1: Alexander, uniformed as a senior officer of the Companions

From the Issus mosaic. On the mosaic the tunic and cloak are a light purplish-grey, but the mosaic was copied from an original painting some centuries old, and all the purples had faded by then. The cloak is damaged in the mosaic, but has been reconstructed with a golden-yellow border by comparison with Plate B3. The green girdle worn over the cuirass, and the green edging to the neck-hole of the shabraque may perhaps have some significance as a squadron colour (of the Royal Squadron?). Normally the king would have worn a Boeotian helmet.

A2: Companion cavalryman

From the Alexander Sarcophagus. Normally the Companion would wear a white cuirass, similar to that of Plate A1 but possibly less ornate. Here a Persian saddle cloth is used in place of the Greek saddle (see Plate C1) and the pantherskin shabraque. Presumably the neck-hole of the shabraque and the cuirass girdle would have been in squadron colours.

B1: Companion cavalryman in hunting dress

From a hunting scene on the Alexander Sarcophagus. This Companion has discarded his body armour for the hunt, and has exchanged his *xyston* for a shorter hunting spear. The lining of the shabraque is red in this case—again, perhaps a squadron colour.

B2: Royal page (?) in hunting dress

Based on a mosaic from Pella showing two youths hunting. Other hunting mosaics show similar cloaks, but in plain white, and the huntsmen use the axe and *kopis* (sabre). A white sun hat is worn, not the *kausia*.

B3: Personal Companion in hunting dress

The colours of the cloaks of the Companion Cavalry are reversed in this figure, which is taken from the Alexander Sarcophagus. It is known that Hellenistic kings would give cloaks to their courtiers or 'Friends' as a special mark of favour; so this huntsman is probably one of Alexander's 'Personal' Companions.

C1: Thessalian cavalryman in hunting dress

From a hunting scene on the Alexander Sarcophagus. Only the short-sleeved under-tunic is worn here, the long-sleeved over-tunic being discarded. The shaggy felt saddle cloth is coloured purple and yellow: the purple (of the same dark shade as the cloak) could be the regimental colour of the Thessalians, and the yellow a squadron colour. Note that the harness is medium brown, and not the red which may have been confined to the Companions.

C2: Officer of Thessalian Cavalry
The laurel wreath around the helmet, either painted on or more probably applied in silver, maybe a mark of rank; the same is almost certainly true of the bracelets. The edge of the cloak is obscured on the Sarcophagus, and has been restored as white by comparison with Plate C1. The colours of the cuirass are difficult to determine. Mendel describes it as yellow, but the watercolours of Winter show the *pteruges* as white faced with fine black lines, and this is supported by personal observation and by comparison with Plate A1. The colours of the back-plate are shown as red and white by Winter, but the precise colouration is lost.

D1: Cavalryman of the 'Prodromoi'
Based on a wall painting from the 'Kinch tomb' near Naoussa, This figure shows a light cavalryman in the last years of Philip's reign. Alexander probably replaced the 'Phrygian' helmet with a bronze Boeotian helmet, and substituted a *sarissa* for the *xyston* shown here. The boots and the hem of the tunic are restored. Parts of the helmet are damaged too, but the lappet flowing from under the rim probably belongs to a helmet liner.

D2: Infantryman in camp dress
This figure is loosely based on a figure from a hunting scene on the Alexander Sarcophagus, wearing only a cloak wrapped round his arm. This is the *ephaptis*, the military 'wrap-around' cloak, used by the heavy infantry. This versatile garment, a long, narrow rectangle of cloth, was normally simply draped over the left shoulder, but could be wrapped round the arm to form a makeshift shield if the soldier went hunting, or got into a fight in camp or town. The tunic is restored, as is the *kausia*—its white colour is guesswork, and blue would also be a suitable colour for the infantry. The axe is restored from a mosaic hunting scene at Pella.

D3: Foot Companion in hunting dress
Restored from a half-naked figure in a battle scene on the Sarcophagus. The tunic has been restored in purple, the colour of the *ephaptis* shown on the Sarcophagus; and it allows us to speculate that this

man could be from the same battalion as Plate G2. He is an officer or a senior soldier; the plumes on his helmet are restored.

E1: Hypaspist
From the Alexander Sarcophagus. The upper part of the helmet is obscured in the original, and is restored here. The bronze shield has a deep purple central medallion on the Sarcophagus, but nothing can be made of the device. The boots are similar to those worn by the cavalry.

E2, E3: Unidentified unit (Allied cavalry?)
Both figures come from the Sarcophagus. The helmet of E3 is shown lying behind the figure on the Sarcophagus; that lying next to E2, which is very similar, comes from another scene on the Sarcophagus. The boots worn by both men suggest a cavalry unit, possibly the Allied Horse, but an identification with the Bodyguards is also possible.

F1: Foot Companion
On the Sarcophagus the colours of the shoulder-pieces and the piping on the lower fringe of the groin-flaps are uncertain; and we have also restored the obscured crest of the helmet. The head of Silenos(?) may have been duplicated on a purple background as the shield device of this battalion. The cuirass is not of the standard design; it is richly coloured, but the red tunic does not make us think of an élite battalion.

F2: Greek mercenary in Persian service
He wears a red *exōmis* tunic leaving the right shoulder free, which was normal dress for Greek mercenaries at this time. He has lost his bronze helmet and hoplite shield; this latter would be in plain bronze. Cuirasses were not worn.

F3: Officer of Foot Companions
Based on a figure on the Sarcophagus which seems to represent an officer. The greaves are silvered, and lined with red material to prevent chafing; note also the red garter. The helmet has a gilt spine running along the crest, and plumes, which are restored here. The colours of the shoulder-pieces are uncertain. His shield, shown resting against the wall, is painted with a battalion shield device, the head of an unidentified female deity.

G1: Senior soldier of Foot Companions

From the Sarcophagus; probably a *dekastateros*, *dimoirites*, *dekadarch* or *hyperetes*. The greaves, although indicating a file- or half-file leader, are bronze, not silvered like those of F3. The helmet, though displaying plumes (restored), does not have the gilt spine on the crest. The white spiral painted on the helmet may be the insignia for a *hyperetes*; the 2nd-century tombstone of a *semeiophoros* (standard bearer) of a Ptolemaic infantry unit in Sidon seems to show a similar spiral. The precise outline of this device is uncertain, as the colours have faded; the same is true of the back of the cuirass and the waist belt.

G2: Foot Companion

The purple tunic of this figure, taken from the Sarcophagus, may indicate a soldier of an élite battalion, possibly a battalion of *asthetairoi* or the Elymiotid *taxis* of Coenus.

G3: Servant

On the Sarcophagus the colours of this figure are very faded. The dark purple stripe is fairly certain, but the main ground colour is not: it seems to be a lighter purple similar to that used by the Companion Cavalry, but red is also possible. The status of these servants is unknown, but they may have been Macedonian youths. The ankle-boots are not of standard military type.

H1: Javelinman

No suitable representation of a light infantryman associated with Alexander's army survives. One figure on the Alexander Sarcophagus may possibly be used as a basis for reconstruction, however. He could be a dismounted cavalryman; but if he *is* an infantryman we have to think of him as a light infantryman, for he wears a Macedonian cloak rather than the *ephaptis* of the heavy infantry. The cloak is thrown up over the left shoulder to leave both arms free. Otherwise he is naked: it is possible that the light infantry fought only in cloaks, but the nudity may be a matter of aesthetic presentation, so we have restored a tunic as worn by G3. He may also have worn boots. In the original publication by Hamdy Bey and Reinach (p. 284) the figure is described as striking at the face of a Persian horseman with a javelin, but this is probably a mistake—he seems to be using a sword. The cloak colour is much faded, and could be either a purple of the same shade as that used by the Companions, or red. Purple makes one think of an élite unit—perhaps the Agrianians? The hypothetical nature of all this speculation must be freely admitted.

H2: Unidentified unit (Bodyguard?)

Based on a figure on the Sarcophagus which is shown naked but for helmet and shield. The gilt spine on the helmet, and the plumes (restored), indicate an officer or senior soldier—perhaps greaves and cuirass should also be worn. The tunic could be either purple or red, two-sleeved or an *exomis*. The shield medallion seems to show Alexander dressed as King of Persia. If this is a regimental shield device, rather than a pure piece of propaganda, it might suggest a unit of Bodyguards or Hypaspists rather than Foot Companions.

H3: Allied Greek infantryman

Based on a figure on the Sarcophagus. The shield would have been plain bronze, but may have been painted with the device of the city in which the detachment was raised. The warrior is shown bareheaded apart from a head-band, but his helmet is shown lying at his feet.

Further Reading

Two modern accounts of Alexander's reign, both well-written and generally available, are *Alexander the Great* by Robin Lane Fox (Allan Lane 1973, Omega Books 1975, 1978) and *Alexander of Macedon* by Peter Green (Penguin 1974). Philip's army is dealt with in Chapter XII of *A History of Macedonia, Volume II* by N. G. L. Hammond and G. T. Griffith (Clarendon Press, Oxford 1979). The standard treatment of the use Alexander made of his army is still J. F. C. Fuller's *The Generalship of Alexander the Great* (London 1958), but E. W. Marsden's *The Campaign of Gaugamela* (Liverpool University Press 1964) has added a lot to our knowledge of Alexander's principal campaign. Donald W. Engels' *Alexander the Great and the Logistics of the Macedonian Army* (University of California Press 1978) deals with questions of supply. A good introduction to military dress and equipment during this period and later is given by Duncan Head's *Armies of the Macedonian and Punic Wars*

(Wargames Research Group 1982).

Plutarch's *The Age of Alexander* and Arrian's *The Campaigns of Alexander* are both currently available in Penguin Classics, but anyone wishing to make a detailed study of Alexander's army will eventually be forced to use translations giving the Greek text in parallel. Most of the ancient sources used in this book are available in this form in the 'Loeb Classical Library' Series published jointly by William Heinemann Ltd. and Harvard University Press. Volume 1 of P. A. Brunt's translation of Arrian contains an introduction with many useful notes. The only English translation of Polyaenus currently available (to my knowledge) is the 1793 translation of R. Shepherd, available in reprint from Ares Publishers Inc. (Chicago 1974).

There are some hundreds of scholarly articles concerning various aspects of Alexander's army—too many to list here. Fortunately, though, two commentaries have recently been published covering Arrian and Curtius. Readers wishing to follow the debate in that depth will be able to find further references in these works, which are *A Historical Commentary on Arrian's History of Alexander, Volume I* by A. B. Bosworth (Clarendon Press, Oxford 1980) and *A Commentary on Q. Curtius Rufus' Historiae Alexandri Magni, Books 3 and 4* by J. E. Atkinson (J. C. Gieben, Amsterdam 1980).

BOOK 2

ALEXANDER'S CAMPAIGNS

PERSIA, GREECE AND MACEDON

To understand the place of Alexander the Great in history, it is necessary to consider briefly the course of events that had determined Greek relations with Persia during the previous century and a half. The Greek cities of the Asiatic Aegean coast had been loosely subject to the Lydian kings of Sardis, until Lydia itself was overwhelmed by the meteoric rise of Persia as an imperial power. The Persians, like the Lydians, were on the whole mild masters. Only in 499BC did the Greek cities of the coast rebel, and when they received help from the Greek mainland, the Persian kings, Darius and Xerxes, launched two unsuccessful punitive expeditions against Greece in 490 and 480BC respectively.

The Persian invasions were repelled and the independence of Greece was secure. But the Greek cities soon relapsed into hostilities among themselves, and the long Peloponnesian War between Sparta and Athens (431–404BC), with its shifting patterns of alliance and confrontation, exhausted Greece. If the Persians were unable to take advantage of Greek weakness, it was because they themselves, following the death of Xerxes in 464BC had entered a period of military weakness. Xerxes' immediate successor, Artaxerxes I, showed considerable diplomatic ability, but in 404 Persia lost control of Egypt, and this province was to be recovered for the Persian Empire by Artaxerxes III, with the help of the Greek mercenary leader Mentor, only in 343BC.

In the last years of the Peloponnesian War, the Persian satraps (provincial governors) of Asia Minor, acting sometimes in combination, sometimes independently, alternately lent their support either to Athens or Sparta in a way best calculated to preserve a balance of power and ensure the continuation of the war. The Athenian defeat of 404BC was brought about because Lysander, the Spartan admiral, had been able to rely on Persian money for the equipment and maintenance of a fleet.

But Spartan supremacy soon alarmed the Persians, and an alliance of Persian and Athenian fleets restored the power of Athens by a naval victory at Cnidos in 396BC. Meanwhile, a Greek army of 10,000 men had supported the pretensions of the Persian Prince Cyrus in a war against his brother Artaxerxes II. This army was committed to a march into Mesopotamia and an arduous withdrawal to the Black Sea coast. As a feat of arms the adventure did not escape notice in Greece, and Spartan generals championing the Greek cities of Asia against Persian satraps were encouraged to campaign in the Asian hinterland. But in 386BC, both Sparta and Athens, in return for Persian recognition of their own claims, conceded the right of Persian dominion over the Greek cities of mainland Asia Minor. Even this somewhat cynical peace did not last long, and the pattern of continual warfare in Greece was soon resumed. War was in fact endemic both in Europe and Asia, and the wealth and energies of all states and nations involved was dedicated year after year to acts of violence and destruction, which were not even prompted by any very obvious patriotic motive.

The Rise of Macedon

From this miserable state of affairs, the territory of Macedonia had been largely exempt. Its geographical position and its strategic significance in the first half of the fourth century were of little account in Greco-Persian politics. Notably, it had not been a party to the treaty of 386 which ceded control of the Greek Asian mainland to Persia. That is not to say that the Macedonians were unwarlike. On the contrary, the mixed populations of Macedonia – Greek, Thracian and Illyrian –

Greece and Macedon

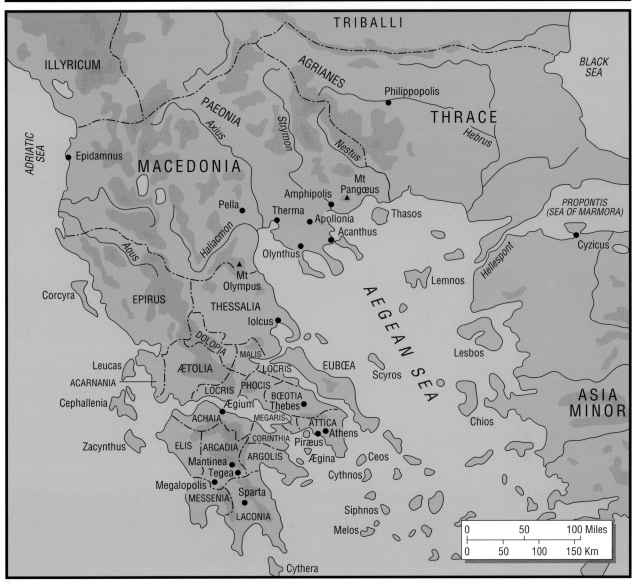

jostled each other and resisted encroaching neighbours.

At last in 358BC, the Greek regent of Macedon made himself king. This was Philip II, father of Alexander the Great. With his seat of government at Pella, some twenty miles north of the Thermaic Gulf, Philip asserted his authority over the whole Macedonian territory and extended his frontiers to embrace the Strymon valley in western Thrace with its ready access to silver mines and gold deposits. Within the next twenty years, by use of political opportunism and a highly trained standing army, Philip was able to dominate the whole field of Greek politics. By imposing on the Greeks a peace they were unable to impose upon themselves, he satisfied that personal ambition which is natural to every able statesman and could at the same time justly be regarded as a benefactor of Greek civilization.

Certainly Philip did not impose himself without a diplomatic and military struggle, which was protracted and often deviously conducted, but when Athens and Thebes at last decided to unite their armies against him, he defeated them sud-

The head of Apollo. as was common on coins of Philip II of Macedon, father of Alexander the Great, and the inscription on the reverse is that of Philip (Philippou). The name Philip literally means 'horse-lover', but we should not suspect a deliberate pun: horse types had long been a feature of Macedonian coins and sometimes derive from those of a Thracian mining district occupied by Alexander I of Macedon (498–454BC).

denly and decisively at Chaeronea in Boeotia in 338BC. Sparta remained aloof. But Philip was able to summon a congress of Greek states to a conference at Corinth, from which he emerged as leader of a Greek federation in war against Persia.

War against Persia had gone far to uniting many of the Greek states at the time of Xerxes' invasion in 480BC. Leading a similarly combined war effort – but this time offensive instead of defensive – Philip could hope to assert his authority over Greece both for its own good and for his. He was, however, assassinated in the year 336, as the result of a domestic plot. Alexander, then twenty years old, executed the murderer without asking questions: perhaps he guessed that the crime had been instigated by his mother, Olympias, in his own interest – for Philip made no pretence to monogamy. At all events, Alexander now inherited his father's kingdom and all that went with it.

Alexander in Charge

Although the war against Persia was for Alexander, as for Philip, a prime political and military aim, he was immediately called to wars nearer home. Philip's pan-hellenic policies had admittedly found friends as well as enemies in Greece. But Alexander's swift descent with his army through Thessaly and Thermopylae (336) was in itself enough to discourage any independent aspirations among the Greek cities, who quickly recognized

him as his father's successor in all that concerned the war against Persia.

Alexander soon made sure that Greece was controlled by Macedonian garrisons or sympathetic politicians. To these latter the term 'puppets' cannot be quite fairly applied: they included sincere men as well as timeservers. In any case, Greece remained tranquil while in 335 Alexander was called away to secure his garrisons in Thrace against rebellion. The tribes in question were receiving help from Scythian allies across the Danube, but Alexander unexpectedly transported his Army across the Danube in local fishing boats and put an end to hostilities on this front. Having the Persian war in mind, he certainly needed to leave Thrace fully pacified, for it lay on the route to the Hellespont (Dardanelles) and the Persian hinterland.

Tribal warfare at this time similarly threatened Macedonia from the Illyrian region adjacent to the Adriatic coast, and Alexander's presence was required in this area also. While he was engaged against the Illyrian tribes, rebellion again broke out in Greece – after a rumour that he had been killed. Two senior officers of the Macedonian garrison in Thebes were murdered and the garrison itself was threatened. When the news reached Alexander, he quickly demonstrated that he was alive, returning to Greece at formidable speed. Even then, he hoped that the Thebans would come to terms, but they did not. He eventually stormed the city and sacked it ruthlessly. Its example was enough to

▲ The Athenian orator Aeschines, contemporary with Philip II of Macedon and Alexander the Great, preserved a conciliatory and compromising attitude towards the Macedonian leadership. This made him for many years the bitter political and personal enemy of Demosthenes. But even in 330BC, when Macedonian power was at its zenith, Demosthenes still got the better of him.

▲ Demosthenes the orator is best remembered for his noble literary style; his career as a statesman is more open to question. Both Philip and Alexander of Macedon showed some forebearance in the face of his relentless hostility. After Alexander's death, he again rallied Athens to the narrow ideals of a Greek city state and, when threatened with arrest by Antipater's Macedonians, committed suicide (322BC).

produce a more conciliatory mood in the rest of Greece, which quickly submitted, as before, to the Macedonian leadership.

Early next spring, Alexander was ready for his war against Persia. He left his commander, Antipater, to guard and garrison Greece with a force of 12,000 infantry and 1,500 cavalry. He himself led his invasion army through Thrace towards the Hellespont. At the most reliable estimate, it was somewhat over 30,000 strong in infantry, including both heavy and light troops, such as archers. The cavalry strength has been

acceptably given as 5,100. Alexander could expect to be joined by other Macedonian troops in Asia, who were the relict of his father's inconclusive war against Athenian satellite cities in Propontis (Sea of Marmara) – though it is likely that many of these troops had by now been withdrawn from the area.

Among Alexander's light troops were notably the Agrianes, a tribal contingent from the extreme north of Macedonia. Alexander, in his war against the Illyrians, had been staunchly supported by Langarus, king of the Agrianes, and Langarus, but

The Conquests of Alexander the Great

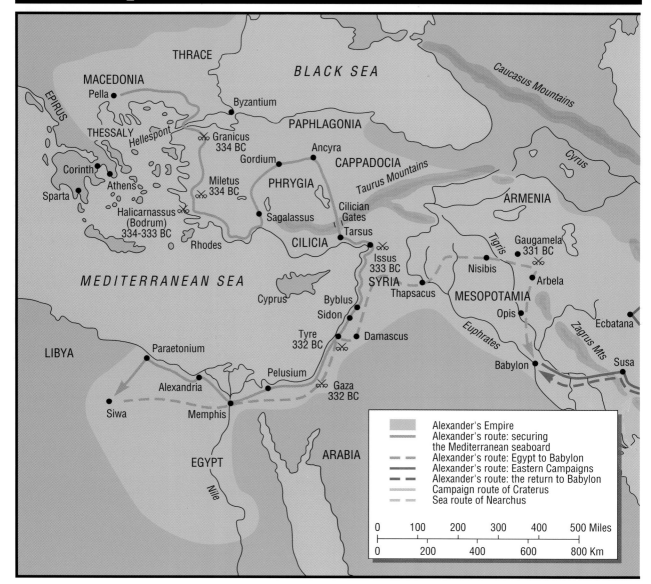

for his untimely death, would have been rewarded by a marriage to Alexander's half sister. In any case, the Agrianes remained among Alexander's most loyal troops. They were to fight in all his major battles in Asia and would follow him to India.

Alexander had thus secured the Greek mainland and Thrace before embarking on his invasion of Persian territory. The precaution was to prove characteristic of him: in the same manner, he later secured the Mediterranean seaboard before penetrating into the Asiatic interior, and he similarly

consolidated his position in Mesopotamia before advancing further east. Nor did he venture on his march to India until the outlying eastern provinces of the Persian Empire were adequately garrisoned. The patience and thoroughness proved by these long-term policies and strategies sorted strangely with a faculty for swift and unpredictable decisions and for actions that often seemed the product of mere impulse. Yet this long-term preparation and forethought underwrote his impetuosity and justified surprise moves that would otherwise have looked dangerously precipitate.

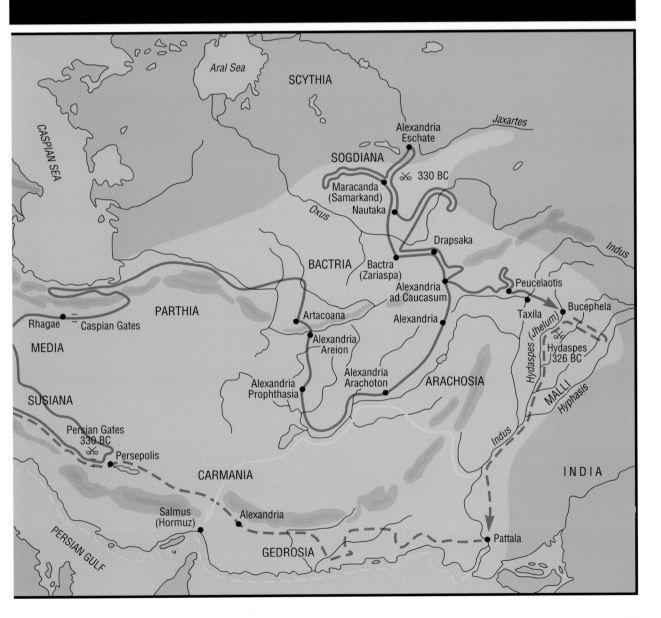

ARMIES AND COMMANDERS

At the outset of his Persian wars and during the four years that followed, Alexander had an able and reliable second-in-command in the person of Parmenio, who had been Philip's trusted general and had led the Macedonian forces on the Asiatic coast against the Allies of Athens. In Alexander's battles, Parmenio regularly commanded the defensive left wing cavalry. He is often represented as giving Alexander advice – which Alexander nearly always rejected.

Parmenio's three sons also served with the Macedonian army under Alexander, Philotas as a dashing young cavalry officer, Nicanor in command of infantry, while Hector was probably still too young for any command. Sadly, Hector lost his life by an accident on a Nile boat, and Nicanor died in the East. Even more tragic ends, with probably unmerited disgrace, awaited Philotas and Parmenio himself. After their death, other officers such as Coenus and Craterus came into prominence, not to mention Seleucus and Ptolemy who, with others, were to be the heirs to Alexander's conquests.

The life of Hephaestion was almost coextensive with Alexander's own life, and he retained Alexander's confidence and affection throughout. Yet he was never a distinguished commander in battle, being mentioned mainly in connection with ancillary services, transport and communications. When he died at Ecbatana in 324BC, Hephaestion left a sorrowing Persian widow and was given a magnificent funeral.

The Persian generals who confronted Alexander in north-west Asia (Arsames, Petines, Rheomithres, Niphates and Spithridates) were slow to mobilize in the face of the Macedonian threat, but Spithridates and other Persian commanders showed impetuous courage in battle. In this respect, they differed from Darius himself, who for all his elaborate warlike preparations, fled from the battlefield precipitately as soon as he was personally threatened.

The Persians were initially aided by Memnon, a commander of Greek mercenaries, brother of that Mentor who had helped to reconquer Egypt for the Persian Empire. Persian jealousy of Memnon, however, led to divided counsels before the Battle of the Granicus.

Men and Weapons

Alexander had inherited from his father the army he led into Asia. On the battlefield, it consisted mainly of three formed bodies: an assault force of right-wing cavalry, defensive left-wing cavalry, and a central mass of infantry pikemen operating usually in contact with those other substantially equipped foot-soldiers known as 'hypaspists'. (A hypaspistes was originally a shield-bearer – often a slave. The word could also refer to a king's honoured armour-bearer. It applied in an honourable sense to Macedonian infantrymen.) To these were added, frequently in wing positions, lightly-armed skirmishing troops – archers, slingers and javelin-throwers. The way in which all these troops were used emerges in the study of individual battles. The élite 'Companion' cavalry were

▶ *This illustration is copied from a silver coin in the British Museum. It is struck in the name of the Persian king, as lettering on the reverse indicates. The head-dress again exhibits the typical side flaps, but it is secured with a band or filet. We may perhaps compare it with that worn by the figure on the extreme right in the Issus Mosaic.*

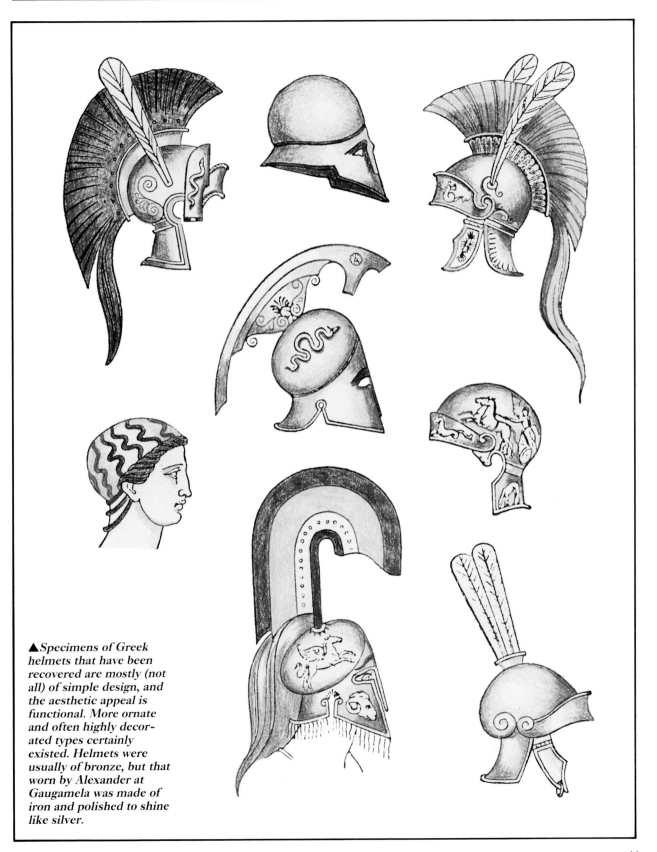

▲ Specimens of Greek helmets that have been recovered are mostly (not all) of simple design, and the aesthetic appeal is functional. More ornate and often highly decorated types certainly existed. Helmets were usually of bronze, but that worn by Alexander at Gaugamela was made of iron and polished to shine like silver.

▼ *A Macedonian hypaspist guardsman. The exact nature of these troops is not clear, but it seems probable that they were lighter troops than the phalangists and protected the vulnerable flank of the phalanx in battle. (Painting by Richard Geiger)*

mainly Greek-speaking Macedonians and they were supported by other non-Greek Macedonian horse squadrons (Paeonians from northern Macedonia) and lancer scouts. Thracian and Thessalian horsemen often served with Parmenio on the left wing.

The Companions were protected by metal helmets and partially metal corselets, but carried no shields. Horsemen of other contingents were more lightly equipped. The helmeted infantry pikemen wore bronze greaves and carried small shields which they manipulated on their forearms. The hypaspists, (sometimes translated 'Guards'), were spearmen who carried conspicuous shields. Both they and the pike soldiers were sometimes described as 'Foot-Companions'. Both were Greek-speaking Macedonians – if allowance be made for an uncouth dialect.

The Companions, whether cavalry or 'Foot-Companions' were recruited from Macedonian localities on a territorial basis. Each was therefore the 'companion' of his neighbour in arms, as of the

▲ *Swords in scabbards were carried by most Greek and Macedonian infantrymen as reserve weapons. The shafts of spears and pikes might easily be broken, and even archers could at any time* *find themselves closer to the enemy than they had bargained for. By Alexander's epoch, the slashing sword ('kopis' or 'machaira') had become common.*

◄ *A Persian 'Apple-bearer' Royal foot guard equipped with a brown leather, bronze-studded cuirass, a Greek-style bronze shield and a Persian infantry thrusting spear counter-weighted by the golden 'apple' that gave the unit their name. (Painting by Richard Geiger)*

▲*Greek sculptors and painters mingled realism and convention in their portrayal of mythological subjects. This statue represents Eros (Cupid) bending his bow; Cupid's use of the leg, with a slightly crooked knee, for testing or stringing a bow was probably normal practice in Alexander's time.*

king or commander whom he served. In which sense the word originally applied is not certain.

Other Macedonians, from the wilder and more remote parts of the territory, served as skirmishers and missile fighters – as already described. They relied for defence on their own unencumbered agility, some of them using light shields. Most troops carried swords in scabbards as weapons of last resort.

Alexander of course led with him Greek and Thracian allies. Greek mercenaries were always available to any general that needed them.

The main strength of the Persian troops who opposed Alexander lay in their horsemen and bowmen. Archers were in fact often mounted, in which case they were protected only by tunics and breeches of quilted material. Heavy cavalry wore corselets, which sometimes resembled those of the

▼ *Various types of ancient spear. One shows a butt weight fitted for balance. The loop attachments in the next have been interpreted as appendages to assist a horseman in mounting, but more probably the shafts in the original ancient reliefs* were intended as those of *javelins, and the loops are thongs such as were used by javelin-throwers to gain distance and force. Alexander made good use of javelin-throwers when confronted by Porus's elephants.*

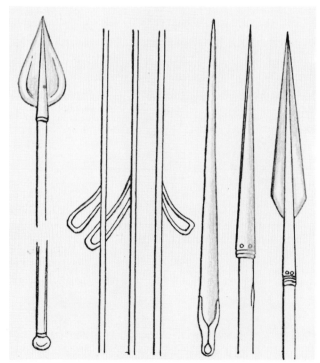

▲*This Persian soldier, from a fourth century vase, is an attendant of King Darius, splendidly dressed in embroidered clothing. His shoes, unlike most ancient Greek footwear, cover the toes. His cap with its side flaps is typical of those worn by the Persians and other non-Greek ('barbarian') nations. It is probably cut* to shape from the skin of *a small animal, the lappets being trimmed from the legs of the skin. When drawn scarf-like across the chin or lower part of the face, these flaps would give protection in battle or hunting, or against flying dust. (Compare with the Issus Mosaic.)*

Greeks but sometimes were made of soft material faced with metal scales.

For infantry, the Persians relied much on Greek mercenary hoplites. They also had their own heavy infantry, probably armed in imitation of the Greek hoplites (called Cardaces). Lighter infantry used spears and thrusting swords, and relied on quilted clothing for body protection. The many national contingents from the far-flung Persian empire probably had no equipment save their ordinary hunting weapons.

War Aims and Strategies

It is very hard to judge how far Alexander's ambitions, at any particular time and place, had already taken shape. One can only stress again that he believed in consolidating his conquests before proceeding to any fresh venture.

His first professed purpose was to liberate the Greek cities of Asia. Later, while he was still subduing the Phoenician cities of the Syrian and Palestinian coast, he stated in a letter to Darius that his aim was to avenge Persian invasions of Greece in the past. Darius offered to cede to him the Persian western dominions, but he rejected the offer, and he was obviously bent in 332BC on invading Mesopotamia.

When this was accomplished he was still unsatisfied. His purpose was to capture the fugitive Darius, and this gave him the pretext for invading the north-east provinces of Persia. It is particularly hard to know whether his aim of blending Persian and Greek civilization and culture should be regarded as an expedient for pacifying conquered territory or a visionary ideal for the political future. Indeed, his motives, as often, may have been mixed.

In 327, when he crossed the Indus and pressed on beyond the frontiers of Darius's empire, his motives can only be explained as marching and conquering for the love of marching and conquering. It is a miracle that men followed him as long as they did – but even Alexander's army rebelled in the end.

It cannot of course be said that Alexander's enemies had any positive or expansionist war aims of their own. Their purpose was merely to defend

▲ *The Greek 'himation' could be used equally as a cloak or blanket. The accompanying illustration from a Greek vase shows a soldier in marching order, his 'himation' fastened with a clasp over his chest. On his head is the broad-brimmed felt hat known as a 'petasus'. His footwear is notably substantial and the leggings are separate from the shoes – the uppers of which are supplied by latticed thongs. Despite the barefooted warriors commonly depicted in battle scenes, it is clear that an ancient army could expect to march well shod.*

themselves against him. In this, all ultimately failed. In all cases, the only alternative was to recognize him at the outset as a friend and ally, offering a contribution of men and materials to his ongoing wars. Even to a conquered foe, Alexander could be generous, but he could also on occasion be extremely savage and vindictive.

THE BATTLE OF THE GRANICUS

In April 334BC, Alexander crossed the Hellespont. While the crossing was being completed by his troops, he visited the ancient site of Troy and ceremoniously sacrificed in honour of the legendary Greek heroes who had, like himself, waged war against an Asian power on Asian soil. For ferrying his army, he used many transport vessels convoyed by 160 war galleys (triremes). His first objective was to liberate the Greek cities of Asia from Persian control, and for this purpose he needed to march southwards along the east coast of the Aegean. However, a large Persian army, which had not arrived in time to prevent his crossing, now threatened him from the east of the Troad. He could not leave it in his rear, and was in any case always glad of the challenge to a pitched battle.

The Persian forces were now encamped at Zelia, and to meet them Alexander advanced across the Troad, a territory intersected by rivers that flowed northwards into the Sea of Marmara (Propontis). One of these, the Granicus, provided a defensive moat for the Persian positions. The Persian King, Darius III, remote in his eastern capital of Susa, had entrusted his army in Asia Minor to the command of the governors of his western provinces. A body of Greek mercenary troops was serving with the Persians, and this was commanded by Memnon the Rhodian, an officer who had already proved his ability in battle against the Macedonian forces. The contingent he now led was slightly under 20,000 strong, a number approximately equal to that of the Persian cavalry. However, he was supported by very few Persian infantry. The Persians were not usually at a numerical disadvantage and one can only assume that the Persian infantry had not yet been fully mobilized. Indeed, the Persian military reaction on this occasion seems in general to have been seriously belated.

Alexander approached the Granicus over country that afforded a degree of early deployment. His main body of heavy infantry marched in two tandem columns with the cavalry guarding its flanks and the baggage train following. Under the leadership of an officer named Hegelochus, a mixed force of scouts, consisting of mounted lancers (sarissophoroi) and 500 lightly armed infantry, reconnoitred the way ahead.

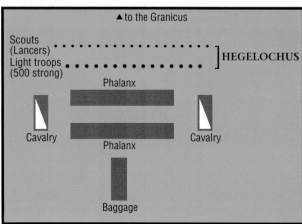

Advance to the Granicus

▲ to the Granicus

Scouts (Lancers)

Light troops (500 strong)

] HEGELOCHUS

Phalanx

Cavalry

Cavalry

Phalanx

Baggage

◀ *This was a position of semi-deployment: the 'double phalanx' could quickly form a square in case of surprise attack. A Macedonian or Greek army advanced in semi-deployment through open country wherever it could. Column of march, where required by a mountain pass, was exposed to sudden flank attack from above. It was a position to be avoided, and Alexander was usually careful to occupy mountain passes with advance guards, well ahead of his main body.*

The baggage followed in the rear. This differed from the practice of Greek armies of an earlier date, where the position of the baggage was often central; Alexander's highly mobile cavalry on the wings would no doubt have been quite capable of confronting and repelling any attack from the rear.

Battle of the Granicus: Alexander on the left bank

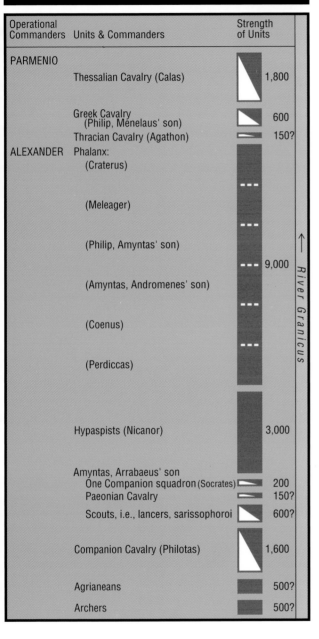

Operational Commanders	Units & Commanders		Strength of Units
PARMENIO			
	Thessalian Cavalry (Calas)		1,800
	Greek Cavalry (Philip, Menelaus' son)		600
	Thracian Cavalry (Agathon)		150?
ALEXANDER	Phalanx:		
	(Craterus)		
	(Meleager)		
	(Philip, Amyntas' son)		9,000
	(Amyntas, Andromenes' son)		
	(Coenus)		
	(Perdiccas)		
	Hypaspists (Nicanor)		3,000
	Amyntas, Arrabaeus' son		
	One Companion squadron (Socrates)		200
	Paeonian Cavalry		150?
	Scouts, i.e., lancers, sarissophoroi		600?
	Companion Cavalry (Philotas)		1,600
	Agrianeans		500?
	Archers		500?

→ *River Granicus*

Battle of the Granicus: The Persian Order of Battle

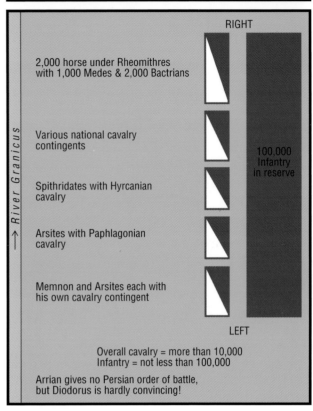

RIGHT

2,000 horse under Rheomithres with 1,000 Medes & 2,000 Bactrians

Various national cavalry contingents

Spithridates with Hyrcanian cavalry

Arsites with Paphlagonian cavalry

Memnon and Arsites each with his own cavalry contingent

→ *River Granicus*

100,000 Infantry in reserve

LEFT

Overall cavalry = more than 10,000
Infantry = not less than 100,000

Arrian gives no Persian order of battle, but Diodorus is hardly convincing!

◀ *The plan shows the deployment of Alexander's army on the left bank of the Granicus, before the battle. Parmenio commanded the left wing. Alexander himself assumed operational responsibility for the rest of the army, eventually taking up his position on the right, with the Companion Cavalry. Amyntas, son of Arrabaeus, was in charge of the assault force that was to open the battle at the river crossing. At the time of the actual crossing, an infantry unit, probably peeled off from the adjacent hypaspists, was added to Amyntas's command. The figures given for the strength of units are those estimated by Professor N. G. L. Hammond in* The Journal of Hellenic Studies, *vol. 100, 1980.*

The Macedonian army was not far from the River Granicus when messengers came back from Hegelochus reporting that the enemy had been sighted drawn up in line of battle across the river. The approach to the Granicus was such that Alexander was able to extend his own army, already half deployed, to form a battle front.

His second-in-command, Parmenio, is at this stage on record as having suggested a waiting policy, arguing that it would be better for the Macedonians to camp that night in their current position. The swift deep river and its craggy banks were a formidable barrier between the two armies, and if Alexander's men now took the initiative in forcing a crossing they would emerge on the opposite bank in scattered groups or in column, in a way that would expose them to dangerous counter-attacks. Parmenio apparently pointed out that the enemy was outnumbered in infantry and would not risk bivouacking near the river bank, where they would be vulnerable to a surprise attack during the night. If the Macedonians waited till dawn and made sure that the farther bank was not yet occupied by the enemy, they might well snatch

▲Most evidence indicates that the 'ephippion' was a mere saddle cloth, attached to no rigid frame. However, it has been argued that such a usage was not invariable. Certainly, horsemen of Alexander's time lacked the advantage of stirrups. The suggestion has been made that horses were trained to kneel at a word of command to permit their being mounted (as in this illustration from an ancient lamp decoration), but Alexander is described as vaulting on to his horse at the Granicus, and any able-bodied cavalryman would have been capable of doing the same.

their opportunity of crossing before the Persians moved up.

Parmenio may actually have spoken in this way, or it may be an ancient historian's manner of dramatizing a military dilemma. But in any case, Alexander is represented as dismissing the idea contemptuously. It was a question of morale: an immediate attack would put courage and confidence into the Macedonians and would daunt the Persians.

Even so, the two armies waited for some time on either side, each hesitating to make a move. The Persians from the high ground they occupied beyond the river were able to observe the position of Alexander himself, distinguishable by his splendid armour and entourage. At a recent council of war held by King Darius's generals, Memnon the Rhodian had been against taking any action at all. He wished to retreat, conducting a scorched-earth policy and depriving Alexander's army of any supplies. It would then be possible to defend the Greek cities of the Aegean coast by a purely naval strategy and Alexander would be isolated from both Asia and Europe. The Persian generals, however, were jealous of the confidence King Darius placed in Memnon, and they were not willing to make the sacrifices a scorched-earth policy would involve. Alexander, for his part, had reason enough for an immediate attack. Quite apart from any question of morale, if he waited, the Persians might receive massive reinforcements and he would lose the advantage of superior infantry numbers he now enjoyed.

Alexander's Tactics

Throughout his campaigns, it may be argued, Alexander used the standard tactics he had inherited from his father Philip. Yet these basic tactics were implemented with astonishing versatility, improvisation and resource, as time and place required. Of such variation on a theme the Battle of the Granicus is an eminent example.

The characteristic Macedonian battle plan depended on coordination of the comparatively static infantry phalanx with a fast-moving cavalry wing, which reached out on the right to outflank and encircle the enemy, ultimately drawing them in against the bristling pike front of the phalanx. The function of the phalanx, in this respect, has been compared to that of an anvil rather than a hammer. But how to carry out such tactics, when in place of the wide plain that was ideally suited to them a steeply banked river, swollen with spring floods, separated the two opposing armies?

Alexander, now leading his right wing cavalry, as was his custom, struggled upstream against a strong current. He was determined as always that he should outflank the enemy, not be outflanked by them. In the hours before the action began, the Persians from their higher positions had been able to watch his personal movements; however, once the attack had been launched with a fanfare of trumpets and loud battle cries and the Macedonian vanguard had entered the river, Alexander and the élite Companion cavalry he commanded must have been screened by the contours of the land, the bends of the river and the trees that grew along its margin.

▲ *The 'salpinx' was a type of military trumpet that was long in use in ancient Mediterranean countries for giving military signals. Its invention is traced to the Etruscans. The Romans used the same type, and its Latin name was 'tuba'. It was long and* *straight, as the illustration shows, and made of bronze. (The 'cornu', a curved horn, was also used in warfare.) Alexander and his Macedonians at the Granicus opened their attack to the sound of the trumpet (salpinx).*

We are not told anything of the part played by Parmenio in this battle. It is merely remarked that at the outset Alexander sent him to take charge of the left wing. In the first stages of the action at any rate, the left wing role may have been purely defensive. There was always some danger that with such heavy cavalry preponderance the Persians would turn the tables on Alexander and counter his encircling movement on the other side of the field with a sally of their own right wing, crossing the river, attacking the baggage camp and presenting the Macedonian centre with a threat from the rear. Parmenio, in overall command of the left wing, including the Thessalian cavalry on the

▲ *This vase illustration shows a hoplite ready for action. He holds out a shallow drinking vessel into which an evidently loving hand pours wine. Inside his big concave shield can be seen the forearm bracket, the* *handgrip, and the lanyard and tasselled pegs used for carrying the shield on a march. The cheek pieces of his helmet are turned up on hinges: he could hear better like that and probably drink more easily.*

Battle of the Granicus: Phase 1
Alexander's Attack

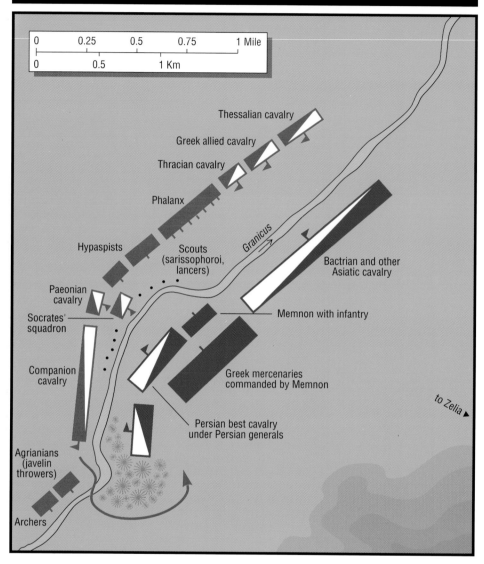

Scale:
0 — 0.25 — 0.5 — 0.75 — 1 Mile
0 — 0.5 — 1 Km

Thessalian cavalry

Greek allied cavalry

Thracian cavalry

Phalanx

Hypaspists

Scouts (sarissophoroi, lancers)

Granicus

Bactrian and other Asiatic cavalry

Paeonian cavalry

Socrates' squadron

Memnon with infantry

Companion cavalry

Greek mercenaries commanded by Memnon

Persian best cavalry under Persian generals

Agrianians (javelin throwers)

Archers

to Zelia ▲

◄ *The frontal attack was led by a squadron (ilē) of the Companions under Socrates, son of Sathon. Socrates' squadron was the leading squadron for that day (apparently by roster). Socrates' attack was made at the main crossing place on the road to Zelia, which was probably kept clear by the Persian authorities for purposes of trade and travel. At this point the two opposing armies were in full view of each other across the river. Socrates had with his own squadron one of Paeonian cavalry (north Macedonian tribal horsemen) and a detachment of infantry, probably drawn from the hypaspists on his left. The mounted lancer scouts, who followed just behind him, must have fanned out at once, to explore the river bank for other likely crossing places. Socrates' men, as they approached the opposite bank, were subjected to showers of enemy missiles. These would have been launched both by Persian mounted bowmen and light-armed Greek mercenaries, at this point under the direct command of Memnon himself. While the frontal assault was being carried out in this way, Alexander rode at the head of his*

extreme left, may have been detailed to hold the line of the river against any such counter-offensive until the Macedonian central attack had so absorbed the enemy's efforts that it was safe for them to cross. Indeed, Macedonian battle tactics always required a strong left wing to balance and safeguard audacious operations on the right.

At the Granicus, the famous infantry pikemen of the Macedonian phalanx formed the centre as usual. Less characteristically, they opened the fighting, a role more commonly assigned to Alexander's Companion cavalry on the right wing.

Even so, the actual spearhead of attack at the river crossing was a cavalry squadron placed in front of the phalanx, having been moved up, it would seem, from the right. As these units reached the opposite bank, they were greeted with volleys of missiles and soon came into full collision with the flower of the Persian cavalry and with Memnon's heavy infantry, who awaited the attackers from a position of advantage. The losses of the Macedonians were predictably serious.

Alexander's officers in the central sector must have known as well as he did that the whole operation was a gamble against time, and the wholehearted dedication shown both by themselves and the men they commanded was a measure of their confidence in Alexander and of their devotion to him. He may have found the river current, as he struggled upstream, stronger than he had expected, but in any case he accepted – as he often did – a calculated risk.

Certainly, the manoeuvre of the Companion cavalry to secure the outflanking position Alexander required was long and circuitous, carrying him far from the main battle centre. This was the cost of trying to encircle a larger force with a smaller force. The Persians, for their part, were evidently taken by surprise as Alexander appeared on their left. This is shown by the precipitate haste with which the Persian commanders transferred their attention from the central action to meet the new threat. One ancient account refers to fierce opposition encountered by Alexander as he scaled the farther bank of the river, but this resistance, if accurately reported, must have been offered by a small detachment posted to guard what was considered a remote and unlikely crossing place.

Persian numbers were such that cavalry could be spared to counter-attack as Alexander ad-

Companions (less Socrates' squadron) into the water, upstream, in a wide outflanking movement. He also had with him archers and Agrianean javelin-throwers. The left wing under Parmenio made no immediate move to cross, but guarded the river bank against any attempted crossing by the enemy.

▶ *The Persian left wing pivoted on to the new battle front which Alexander had opened. As Alexander pressed his attack, the Persian commanders led cavalry from the centre to support their left wing. The Persian transfer of troops from the river bank meant that resistance in this sector was reduced and the Macedonians were able to cross more easily. The intense pressure on Socrates was relieved both by the infantry crossing the river behind him and by Alexander's approach on his right.*

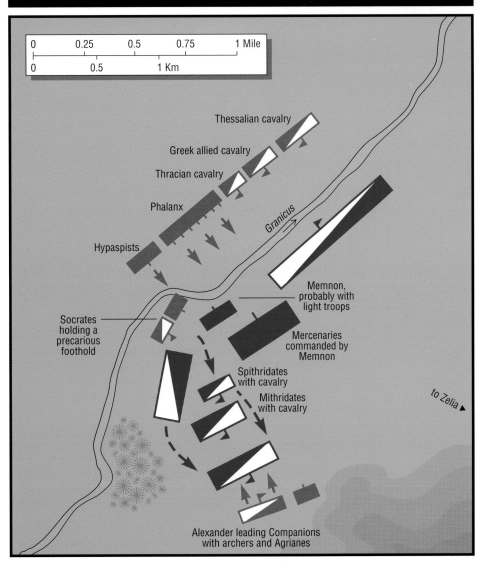

Battle of the Granicus: Phase 2

0   0.25   0.5   0.75   1 Mile

0   0.5   1 Km

Thessalian cavalry

Greek allied cavalry

Thracian cavalry

Phalanx

Granicus

Hypaspists

Memnon, probably with light troops

Socrates holding a precarious foothold

Mercenaries commanded by Memnon

Spithridates with cavalry

Mithridates with cavalry

to Zelia ▲

Alexander leading Companions with archers and Agrianes

vanced, but the short spears of the Persian horsemen were no match for the long Macedonian lances (sarissai). Moreover, the diversion of forces to confront Alexander removed pressure from the desperately threatened Macedonian vanguard at the river's edge. Those who here survived pressed their attack no further, falling back slightly in order to benefit by the impact of Alexander and his Companions on their right.

Meanwhile, as other Persian troops became absorbed increasingly into conflict with Alexander's wing, the banks of the river were less heavily guarded. Wave after wave of Macedonians were now able to cross at various points, reinforcing the bridgehead that had been so precariously established.

The situation that developed was a typical result of Alexander's tactics. The Persian horse was caught between the jaws of an enveloping pincer movement. Here, however, the sheer density of the mêlée to some extent deprived the Macedonian lancers (sarissophoroi) of their advantage. Their long lances easily became entangled and broken. Fighting was hand-to-hand in a way that was more typical of Greek infantry tactics than of cavalry warfare, as horse cannoned against horse. On both sides, swords were drawn, and with the edge of the sword no less than with the point of the lance matters were finally decided.

◄ *Neither the men of the pike-phalanx nor the hypaspists seem to have worn a corselet, as did Alexander's Companion cavalry. Their ordinary dress was the soldier's 'chiton', as shown in the illustration. The phalangists, apart from their shields, relied for defence, as for attack, on their ability to outreach the enemy with their long pikes.*

The First Victory

In the very heart of the battle, the commanders of the opposing forces came face to face. Certainly, nothing could have better suited Alexander's strong sense of drama and taste for epic personal conflict. His lance had snapped, but he shouted to Aretis, an officer of his bodyguard, to give him another. Aretis's lance was also broken, but Demaratus, a Corinthian guardsman, gave him what he needed, and so armed Alexander made his way through the press, for he had caught sight of Mithridates, the son-in-law of King Darius, at that moment leading a wedge-shaped formation of Persian horse into the fray. Mithridates was riding well out ahead of the men he commanded and was to that extent isolated. Alexander saw his opportunity for single combat. He charged, and his lance point took the Persian prince full in the face, hurling him lifeless to the ground.

Rhoesaces, brother of the Persian commander Spithridates, rode up too late to save the fallen man, but still aimed to avenge him. He slashed at Alexander's head with his sword (kopis), and cracked the magnificent helmet – but the blow was turned, and the helmet saved Alexander. He wheeled about and was again able to use his lance, piercing Rhoesaces mortally through the body.

Spithridates was himself now instantly on the spot. Either Alexander had been unable to extricate his lance intact or had no time to level it again, for the Persian was already at sword's length from him and raised his falchion for what would probably have been a fatal stroke. But before the blow could fall, Alexander's trusted officer Clitus slashed at Spithridates' shoulder and hewed it clean off. There are other versions of the same bloody episode; all end with Spithridates, Rhoesaces and Mithridates left dead upon the field.

By this time, the Macedonian cavalry as well as the infantry were able to cross the river at all points with comparative ease, and as these joined the fray the Persians were increasingly forced on to the defensive. They were rolled back from the river bank in some confusion, harassed also by the missiles of archers and javelin-throwers whom Alexander had interspersed among his Companion cavalry.

The newly arrived Macedonian horsemen, who now rallied around Alexander, were able to make good use of their lances, striking at the faces of the enemy and at the heads of their horses. Soon the Persians began to give way, especially in that sector where Alexander himself was personally conspicuous.

Full flight ensued. Indeed, only by flight could the Persians save themselves from being crushed between Alexander's cavalry and the now firmly established infantry phalanx. The Persians had already lost 1,000 horsemen and would have lost more if Alexander had not now turned his attention to Memnon's Greek force.

In contrast, the contingent of Greek mercenaries had retreated to rising ground and defended its position with professional courage. Arrian, the best informed historian of the action, remarks unkindly that the mercenaries had no plan but were simply stupefied by the unexpectedness of the disaster. At one stage, it seems, they sued for honourable terms. But Alexander would grant none. At all events, the whole mercenary contingent was surrounded and ultimately killed or captured, save for a few who escaped by pretending to be dead. Memnon, their leader, escaped – whether or not he did so by feigning death is unrecorded. He lived to serve the Persian King for another year, and, but for his unforeseeable early death from an illness, might easily have become a serious thorn in Alexander's side.

It is reported that 25 of Alexander's Companion cavalry were killed in the battle, and of other cavalry 60. Infantry losses were apparently 30. These figures seem surprisingly low in view of the fierce fighting. Alexander buried the dead of both sides with due honours and indemnified the families of his fallen soldiers with exemptions from taxes and feudal dues. He personally visited all the wounded and listened patiently while they told him of their adventures in the battle.

The 2,000 Greek mercenaries whom he captured were sent back to Macedon in chains under sentence of hard labour. He regarded them as traitors to the united Greek cause of which he claimed to be the legitimate leader. Memnon's men probably never considered that there was such a thing as a united Greek cause, and in their

▲ *This foot-soldier (from a vase at Naples) wields a slashing sword ('kopis'). Such weapons were typical of Greek or Macedonian troops in the fourth century. The helmet also, typically of a late classical period, lacks a nosepiece. The stiff, as distinct from flowing, crest is characteristic of earlier Greek usage, but this one has a conspicuous flowing tail. Sometimes long hair was confined by a filet and tucked under the helmet. Traditionally, Spartans did not grow their hair long before reaching manhood; Athenian boys, on the contrary, cropped their hair only when they grew up.*

view perhaps a Greek owed no more allegiance to the King of Macedon than to the King of Persia.

To Athens, Alexander remitted a prize of Persian arms and armour for dedication in the temple of the goddess Athena. In an accompanying inscription it was proclaimed that these spoils had been taken by Alexander and the Greeks (with the exception of the Spartans) from the Persians in Asia. The Macedonians, of course, were not specifically mentioned, since Alexander always insisted on considering them as Greeks. The sour reference to the Spartans underlined their sulky abstention from the Congress of Corinth and the

Persian war it had authorised.

He forgave the citizens of Zelia for quartering the enemy army. He saw reasonably enough that they had had no choice in the matter. Other localities in the area, perhaps encouraged by his clemency, easily admitted his officers. The Persian garrison of Dascylion, an important administrative centre, had already fled, and Parmenio was sent to occupy it. Alexander was now free to advance southward and enter Sardis, which had been the headquarters of Spithridates, the ancient Lydian capital from which the Greek cities of the eastern Aegean were controlled.

◄ *This silver coin was from Magnesia on the River Meander in Asia Minor. It was one of those Greek cities which submitted promptly to Alexander after the battle of the Granicus and was occupied by Parmenio. The horseman here depicted is well-armed and wears some kind of boots. The coin is of third-century date. Such cavalrymen served in the armies of Alexander as well as of his successors. No inference should be drawn from the length of the spear, which is here limited by the circumference of the coin, but it seems to have no butt-spike or balancing weight.*

Battle of the Granicus: Phase 3

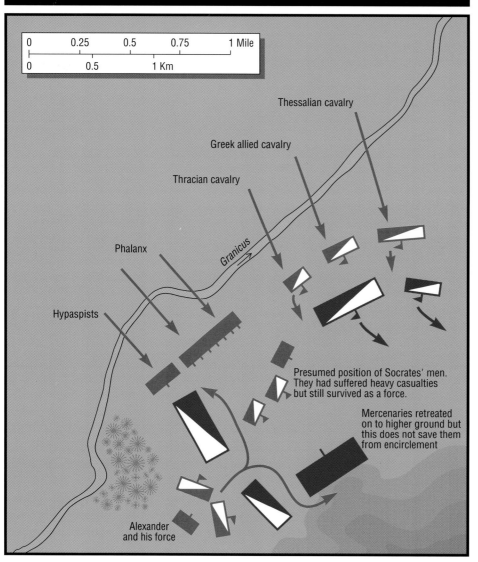

| 0 | 0.25 | 0.5 | 0.75 | 1 Mile |
| 0 | 0.5 | | 1 Km | |

Thessalian cavalry

Greek allied cavalry

Thracian cavalry

Phalanx

Granicus

Hypaspists

Presumed position of Socrates' men. They had suffered heavy casualties but still survived as a force.

Mercenaries retreated on to higher ground but this does not save them from encirclement

Alexander and his force

◄ *After the deaths of Mithridates and Spithridates, the Persian left wing gave way before Alexander's onslaught. The archers and Agrianes, here shown as following Alexander, actually mingled in the cavalry fighting and inflicted damage on the enemy. Alexander had now so far relieved pressure at the centre that the main Macedonian army was able to cross the river and attack both the Persian cavalry and the Greek mercenary infantry that supported it. The Persian left wing, exposed by the crumbling of the centre, is shown in flight, while the Greek mercenaries have retreated on to rising ground, where they will be surrounded and annihilated. Memnon escaped; Socrates survived.*

AFTER THE GRANICUS

After the battle on the Granicus, Alexander appeared, as he had intended to appear and as he saw himself, the liberator of the Greek cities of Asia (liberation in practice meaning the replacement of Persian overlordship by his own). A move in this direction was of course his obvious next step. Whether he already viewed it as the first step in a grand strategy of world conquest cannot be known. He was in the habit of keeping his own counsel until the moment came for action, by which time his mind was already made up.

Liberation on Alexander's terms was now evidently more acceptable to the provincial Persian government than to some of the Greek city states who were the object of his benevolent intentions. Sardis opened its gates to him at once and he was accepted on amicable terms by the Persian

▲ A 'pelta' (peltē) was a light shield of wicker or hide, often of crescent shape, like that in the illustration. Troops for whom the pelta afforded sole protection were common among the Balkan peoples with whom Greeks and Macedonians came into early contact. Similar lightly armed troops were later used in Greece. But after innovations introduced by the

Athenian commander Iphicrates (415–353BC), the Greek peltasts of the late fourth century were more substantially equipped. Note the heavy butt-spike, which enabled the spear to be bedded upright without fear of blunting the head. Alexander's light troops must have included peltasts who were comparable to Balkan mountaineers rather than to Iphicrates' men.

garrison commander. When, however, he turned his attention to those Greek cities of the east Aegean coast that had been administered from Sardis, he met with a varying reception. Ephesus surrendered easily enough. He conferred on it a democracy, subject, of course, to his own suzerainty, and when the pre-existing pro-Persian oligarchy was duly massacred, it was to Alexander's credit that he swiftly intervened to halt mob-rule.

Memnon, having survived the battle on the Granicus, was now active on the Aegean seaboard, conducting the kind of naval warfare that he had advocated before the battle. His plan at that time had been to supply and support the Greek coastal cities against the Macedonians, while laying waste the hinterland and so depriving Alexander's army of sustenance. As it was, he was only able to put half his strategy into action. Alexander remained well supplied on land. Arsites, the Persian satrap who had opposed a scorched-earth strategy at the Granicus, had also survived the battle, but he had committed suicide – he had perhaps too late seen the error of his own judgment.

Miletus, south of Ephesus, would no doubt have surrendered easily enough to Alexander, but with the Persian fleet, which contained substantial Phoenician and Cyprian contingents, close at hand to support resistance, Hegesistratus, the commander of the garrison, was understandably anxious to take sides with a likely winner. Alexander's fleet of 160 warships arrived first and anchored off the island of Lade opposite the city. Alexander stationed his Thracian and 4,000 other mercenary troops on the island, but when the Persian fleet of 400 ships berthed opposite him under the promontory of Mycale on the mainland, he did not risk a sea fight against such numerical odds. Rejecting a compromise solution from the Miletus garrison and citizens according to which the city would be open to Macedonians and Persians alike, he brought up his siege engines. He had already been allowed to occupy the outer city unopposed before his brief parley with the Milesian representatives had taken place.

Alexander's ships now slipped across from Lade and blocked the entrance of the city harbour, anchored in line abreast to cut off the defenders from any hope of seaborne relief. As the besiegers closed in, some of the garrison tried to save themselves by swimming, and 300 Greek mercenaries reached a high rocky island not far out at sea; after capturing the city, Alexander assaulted this island with scaling ladders mounted on boats. He admired the desperate courage of the mercenaries, however, and, sparing their lives, took them into his service. This signalled a new and wiser policy towards Greek mercenaries. The harsh example he had made of those captured at the Granicus might otherwise in future have only have left desperate men more desperate.

The inland cities of Magnesia and Tralles had yielded to Alexander without a struggle, but Halicarnassus on the Carian coast, 100 miles south of Ephesus, was accessible to support from the sea, and Memnon was soon within its walls, sharing command of the garrison with the Persian Orontobates. The city was attacked and defended by every means known to the siegecraft of the ancient world: moats were filled in, towers sapped, walls shaken with rams. The defenders built an interior containing-wall where a breach was threatened and retaliated against siegeworks with fire darts and incendiary sallies. But Alexander continued to inflict heavy casualties and damage, until at last under Memnon's leadership the garrison set fire to its stores and fortifications and escaped southwards. Memnon himself moved north again and occupied Chios, where the Greek population, like himself, saw no particular reason for acknowledging Macedonian rule in preference to Persian. King Darius had by now appointed the Greek mercenary leader supreme commander of all Persian forces in lower Asia. There is an interesting postscript to Alexander's capture of Halicarnassus. In the past, the city had traditionally been governed by one of those matriarchal regimes in which sovereignty was reserved, in the

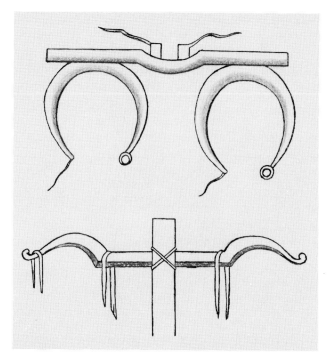

▲ These illustrations of yokes for draft animals occur in medieval manuscript copies of ancient texts. However, they may well be derived from ancient representations. The yoke that fitted over the necks of the animals would be attached to the shaft by a pin or by a knot. Alexander was challenged to fulfil a prophecy by loosening such a knot at Gordium in 333BC. Foreseeing difficulty, he drew his sword and cut the strands: hence our expression 'cutting the Gordian knot' to describe a drastic solution. The story about Alexander may or may not be true, but it is at least in character!

most exclusive manner, for the descendants of a certain family by the marriage of brothers to sisters. In 334BC a female royal claimant called Ada, whose power, curtailed by dynastic quarrels, prevailed only in neighbouring Alinda, welcomed Alexander and offered to adopt him as her son. He accepted the offer and established her eventually as queen of all Caria, including Halicarnassus.

Alexander, meanwhile, did not trouble to pursue Memnon, but was content to secure his own position. He sent home on compassionate leave some of his soldiers who had been newly married before their departure. He also dispatched one of his officers on a recruiting drive to the Greek Peloponnese. That winter, he led his army onward round the south-western extremity of Asia Minor, where the cities and their mercenary garrisons surrendered to him without resistance. He then marched northward on an exploratory expedition to Gordium, where he joined forces with Parmenio, who had already (on instructions) occupied the area. Here also, he was rejoined by the Macedonians who had returned from leave and by new levies from Macedonia and the Greek mainland: 3,000 infantry and 300 horse, all Macedonian, with 200 Thessalian horse and 150 Peloponnesian mercenaries under their own commander.

It was now that Memnon died. His death was an obvious loss to the Persian government and perhaps did more than anything to persuade King Darius that he must now take the field in person against Alexander.

▼*After his victory on the Granicus, Alexander marched southwards and captured those Greek cities which resisted him, including Halicarnassus. The Mausoleum at Halicarnassus, here shown reconstructed, was one of the wonders of the ancient world. Mausolus, the king whose remains it enshrined, was the brother of Queen Ada, Alexander's ally and protégée.*

THE BATTLE OF ISSUS

The strategy and tactics of Alexander's next great pitched battle will hardly be appreciated without some attention to geography. The battle was fought at a point where the Syrian coast meets that of southern Asia Minor at right-angles, in the neighbourhood of Iskanderun (Alexandretta), a name derived from that of Alexander which still preserves his memory. Bearing in mind the map, one is obliged to notice the pattern of strategic marching which preceded the fighting.

March and Counter-March

Events in the Aegean region had at last spurred the Persian king to take the field himself with an army of about 600,000 men. Modern historians have accused ancient historians in general of exaggerating the number of troops deployed by Persian and other oriental potentates with whom Greek and Macedonian armies at different times conflicted. It must be remembered, however, that Persian armies were like modern armies, depend-ing on long lines of communication and supply; Greek armies, by contrast, were small, living on the land over which they marched. Alexander's army was eminently of this kind. The figures given in the present instance for Darius's army may well take account of supporting troops; even so, Alexander, with a force that had crossed the Hellespont no more than 40,000 strong, was clearly outnumbered by a substantial margin.

Darius perhaps believed that his mere numbers would be sufficient to strike terror into the hearts of the Macedonians and their leader, and that the very news of his approach would cause Alexander to flee. Such at least was the opinion the less prudent of his advisers managed to confirm in him. In Darius, apparently, the wish was father to the thought, and his officers and courtiers knew the futility of telling him something he did not wish to hear. Indeed, so great was his optimism that he hoped not merely to drive Alexander from Asia but to trap him there. His only problem, as he saw it, was to prevent the Macedonian army from escaping.

As Alexander marched southwards over the Taurus mountains, to enter the plain near Tarsus by that narrow mountain defile known as the 'Cilician Gates', Darius led his army up the Euphrates valley and across into Syria. He had wished to prevent Alexander from occupying Tarsus and therefore sent his officer Arsames to

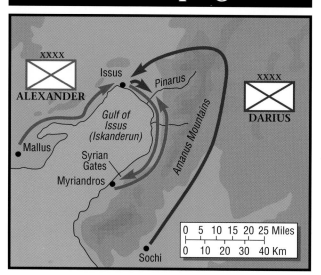

The Issus Campaign

XXXX

ALEXANDER

Issus

Pinarus

XXXX

DARIUS

Gulf of
Issus
(Iskanderun)

Mallus

Amanus Mountains

Syrian
Gates

Myriandros

Sochi

| 0 | 5 | 10 | 15 | 20 | 25 Miles |

| 0 | 10 | 20 | 30 | 40 Km |

◀ The map is purely diagrammatic. Alexander in fact returned from Myriandros towards Issus by the same route that he had followed on his southward march. Darius moving northward from Sochi, was able to bypass Alexander's army unobserved because a mountain range at this stage separated the two opposing forces. The calculations behind these moves are explained in the account of the battle: Alexander did not march north from Myriandros until he knew that Darius was at Issus.

▶ *Alexander's army bivouacked in the mountain pass. In the morning they moved on, along the narrow coastal strip of low ground, the cavalry bringing up the rear. As the lowland strip widened, some deployment became possible: cavalry was brought out to the wings. The infantry line (right to left) was: three units of hypaspists under Nicanor; phalanx units under Coenus, Perdiccas, Meleager, Ptolemy, and Amyntas respectively; left-wing infantry was commanded by Craterus; Parmenio was in overall command of the left wing. Thessalian and Paeonian (?) cavalry was now posted on the right; Greek mercenary troops were sent to the left. These included Cretan archers with Thracian cavalry, both under Sitalces. The left-wing cavalry was mainly allied (Greek). The Thessalians were now brought round the rear to strengthen the left wing cavalry. On the right were Protomachus' scouts with Paeonians under Ariston and archers under Antiochus. Attalus with archers and some cavalry drove off the flanking threat in the mountains. Last-minute moves: two squadrons of horse, under Peroedas and Pantordanus respectively, were moved out from centre to right. A line of Agrianes and Greek mercenaries was used to outflank the Persian left.*

Persian positions during Alexander's advance: a screen of 30,000 cavalry and 20,000 light infantry was thrown forward, south of the River Pinarus, to protect Darius's main body while it was being deployed for battle. When deployment was complete, this advanced line was withdrawn and used mostly to reinforce the Persian right wing, now confronting Parmenio. Darius's front thus consisted of 30,000 Greek mercenaries and 60,000 'Kardakes' (probably lightly armed Persian infantry); the latter were posted on either wing of the Greeks. Behind these forces were ranged the multinational contingents of Darius's imperial army. He himself rode in his war-chariot in the centre.

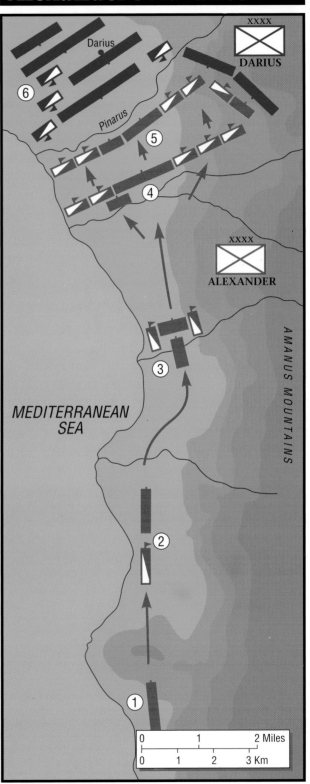

Battle of Issus: Alexander's Advance

hold the Cilician Gates against the invader. But Arsames, supported by an inadequate force, was here faced by a lightly armed and highly mobile detachment commanded by Alexander in person. Arsames did not offer battle and would have burnt Tarsus to prevent it falling into enemy hands, but Alexander was too quick for him, and Tarsus was saved.

At Tarsus, Alexander fell ill from a fever, and the delay this illness occasioned encouraged Darius in the belief that the Macedonians feared a pitched battle. He had encamped at Sochi in Syria, on or near the site of what was later to become Antioch. When he learned that Alexander was still advancing, his first thought was to remain

in his present position. In the Syrian plain, Persian numbers could be used to their best advantage. He would probably have done better if he had adhered firmly to this strategy, but as the situation developed, the opportunity for a master-stroke seemed to present itself.

Alexander, having encamped with his army at Mallus in Cilicia, passed through the coastal defile towards Syria and advanced on the small port of Issus, which had already been occupied by a detachment under Parmenio. A temporary base was here established, in which the Macedonian sick and wounded were left. Alexander then marched southwards along the narrow low-lying coastal strip that separated the mountains from the sea, making for the 'Syrian Gates' near modern Iskanderun.

Possibly he marched at night, as he had done in his swift advance on the Cilician Gates. But this time he led the main body of his army, not merely a mobile striking force. Darius may have been deceived, seeing here a replica of the Macedonian strategy in Cilicia. He resolved on his master-

▲ This sculptured relief shows the god Ares (Mars) in battle against giants. He protects himself with a large, heavy hoplite shield such as was typical of Greek warfare in the Classical period. However, such shields were still used in the second half of the fourth century, and Greek mercenaries, both in Macedonian and Persian pay were probably equipped with them.

stroke: by a circuitous march he would separate Alexander from his local base at Issus and isolate him from the main body of his army. This operation was made easier by a sudden violent storm, which halted Alexander at Myriandrus, on the coast, near the Syrian Gates. Darius took advantage of a valley route just east of the Amanus mountain range and led his army northward again, thus avoiding Alexander's army and by-passing the coastal strip. His manoeuvre, however, had the disadvantage that it brought the Persian army back into the narrow lowland area between sea and mountains, sacrificing the much wider Syrian plain where its numbers could have been more effectively deployed.

Alexander was certainly surprised at the move and sent a trireme up the gulf of Issus to confirm the report that had reached him. In fact this new development came as a pleasant surprise: nothing could have pleased Alexander more than the prospect of a battle on a narrow battlefield. Darius, on the other hand, must soon have been disappointed. When he descended from the mountains near Issus, he found there no more than a hospital base. The Persians massacred many of the Macedonian sick and wounded and ensured a non-combatant role for others by cutting off their right hands. This was perhaps only to be expected – Darius could not at this critical juncture afford to give quarter.

Meanwhile, Alexander with his entire army had wheeled about and was retracing his steps northward. Darius perhaps still considered that he was 'trying to escape' and accordingly advanced the Persian army south of Issus to block his way. When the two forces met, they were separated by the River Pinarus, a narrow torrent bed in which comparatively little water now flowed. Alexander faced north and Darius south.

Superficially, the situation was not very different from that which had existed at the Granicus. But the fact that the Granicus had been swollen with spring floods and that the Pinarus in late autumn now ran low meant that this battlefield was of another kind. Nevertheless, Alexander at once prepared to implement standard Macedonian tactics, with their effective coordination of infantry centre and cavalry wing. As he marched slowly and deliberately northward, the slender margin of coastal lowland widened slightly, and he was able to deploy his army in stages, advancing at last in line of battle.

Face to Face

Darius had been persuaded that Alexander would not of his own accord seek a pitched battle, so he must now have been taken aback. His attitude was in any case defensive. He fortified the already steep bank of the river with a stockade at some points and sent 30,000 horsemen and 20,000 light infantry across the river bed to screen his positions while his battle line was forming. He commanded

30,000 heavily armed Greek mercenaries, and these with 60,000 Persian mercenary troops now constituted the centre of his vanguard, in which position they would confront the Macedonian phalanx. Darius certainly had with him a much greater number of Asiatic foot-soldiers than his generals had commanded at the Granicus. These he posted in large bodies in support of his forward troops, stringing them out in line as far as the narrow battlefield would permit – the sea was not far distant on his right, and the hills were on his left. In the centre of this rather motley array, Darius himself rode in his chariot. The central position was normal to Persian kings in battle, and from it they were able to dispatch orders in one direction or another, to any part of their usually large armies. At Issus, the contours of the foothills were such that the Persian line actually curved forward, posing an encircling threat to Alexander's right wing. In the centre, the Asiatic infantry units, drawn up according to the various localities from which they had been recruited, were so densely mustered that they could not easily be brought into

▼ *This Persian infantry bowman, from a vase painting in the British Museum, looks awkward and ineffectual; but lack of skill should no doubt be imputed to the artist rather than to the archer. The bowman's left,* *leading leg is protected by a pad of some kind and the flap of his 'gorytos' (in Scythian style) hangs down over his thigh. The inscription names the maker of the vase, 'Hischylos'.*

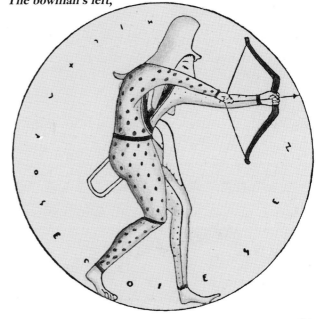

action. The 600,000 men attributed as a grand total to Darius's army, even if not an exaggeration, need not have been actually present on the battlefield.

In Alexander's advancing army, all troops left of the central phalanx were under command of Parmenio. On the right, archers and lightly-armed Agrianes were sent to dislodge the outflanking enemy on the foothills. This was done very easily, and Darius's infantry were quickly dispersed, seeking refuge higher up the mountains, where they posed no threat; nevertheless, 300 of Alexander's horsemen were detailed to watch them.

At the last moment, Alexander withdrew two cavalry squadrons of his Companions from a comparatively central position and sent them to reinforce his right wing. This readjustment was no doubt much needed, for he had already moved the Thessalian cavalry from its original right wing position to his left, where the Persians were massing. Indeed, Darius, as soon as he had been able to retract his cavalry screen from across the river, had concentrated these horsemen on his right against Parmenio. The plain here, close to the sea, no doubt seemed to favour cavalry combat. Both Alexander's late readjustments were made unobtrusively. The Thessalians rode around the rear of the advancing army, and the Companion cavalry, warned that the enemy must not observe them, apparently found cover easily enough among the spurs that extended seaward from the inland foothills.

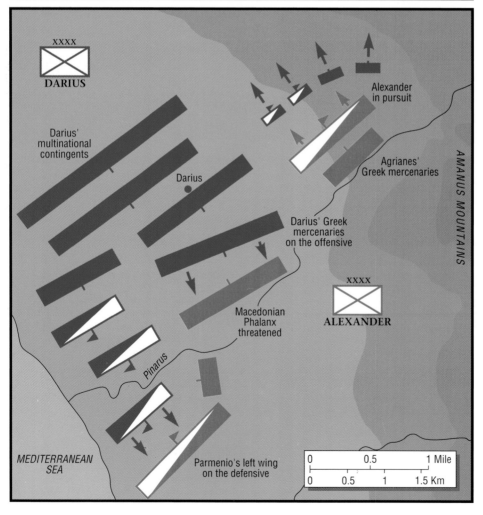

Battle of Issus: The Critical Phase

XXXX
DARIUS

Darius'
multinational
contingents

Darius

Alexander
in pursuit

Agrianes'
Greek mercenaries

AMANUS MOUNTAINS

Darius' Greek
mercenaries
on the offensive

Macedonian
Phalanx
threatened

XXXX
ALEXANDER

Pinarus

MEDITERRANEAN
SEA

Parmenio's left wing
on the defensive

0		0.5		1 Mile
0	0.5		1	1.5 Km

◀ *As Alexander routed and pursued the Persian left wing, there was a danger that the gap between his victorious cavalry and the central phalanx would be exploited by Darius's Greek mercenaries. Parmenio was also on the defensive; and there was a further danger that he might lose touch with the central phalanx and be isolated.*

Alexander continued his slow advance, making sure that the whole army preserved a level front, until he was within missile range of the Persian lines. He then suddenly launched his attack on the right, himself personally leading his Companion cavalry across the river bed and driving back the enemy opposed to him. But in a way typical of ancient battles, the right wing's success carried it forward and out of touch with the centre. The steep and unequal banks of the river, not to mention Darius's stockades, here made it particularly difficult for the phalangists to keep abreast of each other – let alone with Alexander. Into the gap between Alexander's cavalry and the Macedonian phalanx, Darius's Greek mercenaries now penetrated. They would thus soon be in a position to force the phalangists back into the river and threaten from the rear the Macedonian cavalry that had routed the Persian left. One cannot also help suspecting that the gap in the Macedonian line had opened at this point partly as a result of Alexander's last-minute decision to reinforce his right wing cavalry at the expense of his centre. But risks had to be taken somewhere.

The Tides of Battle

In spite of all hazards, the fighting quality of the Macedonian centre was equal to the occasion, although it suffered some 120 significant casualties, and Ptolemy, son of Seleucus, one of its senior commanders, was killed. In the upshot, the

▶ *Alexander, confident that the Persian left wing was shattered irrecoverably, was able to bring relief to this threatened centre. This in turn relieved pressure on Parmenio's left wing, and the whole Macedonian army was able to go forward again. Before long, Darius's army, like Darius himself, was in full flight.*

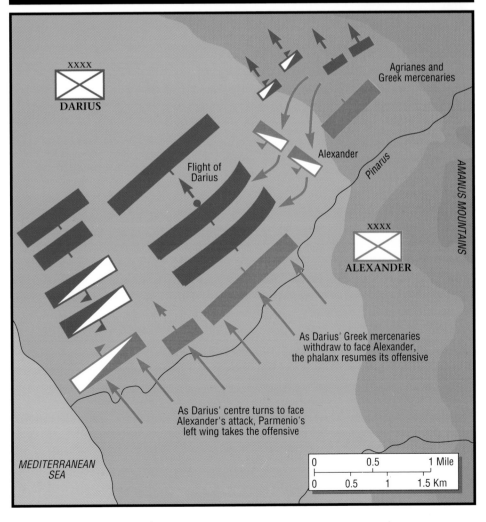

Battle of Issus: The Turn of the Tide

DARIUS

Agrianes and Greek mercenaries

Flight of Darius

Alexander

Pinarus

AMANUS MOUNTAINS

ALEXANDER

As Darius' Greek mercenaries withdraw to face Alexander, the phalanx resumes its offensive

As Darius' centre turns to face Alexander's attack, Parmenio's left wing takes the offensive

MEDITERRANEAN SEA

0		0.5		1 Mile
0	0.5	1		1.5 Km

Macedonians fought off the dangerous counter-attack and managed to contain the salient that had developed on their right, until Alexander was able to come to their aid.

He, for his part, was in full control of the horsemen under his immediate command and did not allow them to make the common mistake of carrying pursuit too far and losing contact with the main battle theatre. Realizing that the Persian left wing was now shattered beyond hope of recovery, he swung round and charged the central body of Greek mercenaries on its flank, forcing them to retreat from the river or cutting them down where they stood. The Macedonian phalanx was then able to advance once more, destroying most of those enemy elements who had survived the impact of Alexander's cavalry.

Darius's army came nearer to success on its right, against the Macedonian left wing where Parmenio commanded. Here, on the sea beach and on the lowland plain adjacent to it, an overwhelming preponderance in cavalry numbers could most obviously be turned to advantage. Whether the Persian right wing cavalry on this occasion took its orders directly from Darius is not clear, but in any case its officers in this sector were reasonably impatient of their purely defensive role, and the Persian horsemen had soon surged across the river to attack the Thessalian cavalry ranged against them. Desperate fighting here took place, but when the Persian right wing saw that the centre and left of their army had collapsed, they wavered and took to flight. No one could blame them. Any attempt to stand their ground must only have led to encirclement by the Macedonian phalanx and Alexander's victorious cavalry. But the very reversal of movement, with the abandonment of headlong pursuit in some quarters for a general headlong flight, in itself threw them into confusion and exposed them to the Thessalians, who now pursued.

The rout of Darius's army in this sector soon became catastrophic. Many of the fugitives were heavily armed and equipped horsemen. Either they were encumbered in their flight or, discarding their weapons, were helpless when overtaken. As they converged in mountain defiles amid increasing panic, horses often fell with their riders, and

▲This famous mosaic, generally agreed to represent the battle of Issus, was discovered amid the ruins of Pompeii, and it is thought to have been based on the work of an original painter almost contemporary with Alexander. When all allowance has been made for the requirements of artistic composition, there is much to be learnt from the picture's realism.

many were trampled to death by those who pressed on from behind. For Parmenio's pursuing cavalry did not relax its pressure, and the fleeing Persian foot-soldiers, who had been posted behind their own cavalry, now suffered equally with the horsemen.

Darius did not wait long enough to see the defeat of his right wing. The moment that his left had crumbled before Alexander's onslaught, he had taken to flight in his chariot, which carried him swiftly enough as long as the ground was level. But when he found himself amid the rocky gorges that lay eastward and northward, he abandoned his chariot together with various weapons and items of clothing, riding now on horseback. It is also

reported that the horses that drew his chariot had been wounded and become unmanageable and that the horse he ultimately mounted had been led behind his chariot for just such an emergency as the present. Nightfall in any case saved the Persian king from Alexander's relentless pursuit.

Ancient historians tell us of 100,000 dead among Darius's troops at Issus and of 10,000 cavalry casualties. It would in any case seem likely that considerably more were killed in the rout that followed the battle than in the actual course of the fighting – a circumstance not uncommon in ancient warfare. It has been noted that Alexander prudently withdrew from pursuit of the enemy before him in order to succour his hard-pressed Macedonian phalanx; however, there was still enough daylight left for him to resume the chase. Darius himself was now the quarry, but Darius's abandoned chariot and equipment was all that immediately rewarded him.

As it was, the Macedonian army quickly occupied the Persian camp, where they made prisoners the royal ladies of the King's household, who had accompanied him on his campaign. These included Darius's wife (who was also his sister) with his baby son and his mother. Two of his daughters were also captured, together with some other noble Persian ladies who attended them.

Money, too, had been left behind. Arrian refers rather casually to 'no more than 3,000 talents'. But a comparison is here intended with the much greater spoils that awaited the victors when they occupied the Persian general headquarters at Damascus. One talent was 6,000 drachmas, and eighty years earlier one drachma had been a high daily rate of pay for an Athenian naval oarsman. There was, at Issus, certainly enough to pay and supply Darius's huge field army throughout the anticipated campaign.

Alexander treated with great chivalry the Persian ladies who had fallen into his power. When they believed that Darius was dead and wept hysterically, Alexander himself reassured them,

▼A Greek mercenary in Persian service. He wears the standard panoply for a hoplite, including a long thrusting spear, a later version of the 'Chalcidian' helmet and stiffened leather or linen armour. The large 'Argive' shield is augmented by a leather apron to give additional protection from missiles, a threat more common in Asia than in Greece. (Painting by Richard Geiger)

telling them of the King's escape. He had, he said, no personal grievance against Darius but fought merely in pursuit of a legitimate political claim – the control of Asia.

Although wounded in the leg by a sword-thrust, Alexander attended to the honourable burial of the dead and visited all his wounded men, offering consolation and congratulation as it was due, and conferring rewards on those who had merited them in the battle. Meanwhile, Darius continued his flight eastward. He had been joined by other fugitives to the number of about 4,000, and his main intention was to put the River Euphrates between himself and Alexander as soon as possible.

Some 8,000 Greek troops, who had previously deserted from Alexander to Darius, escaped westward. Reaching the Phoenician coast at Tripolis near Mount Lebanon, they found the ships that had originally brought them from Lesbos. Any surplus ships were burnt, lest they should be used by pursuing forces. Some of the fugitives sailed to Egypt via Cyprus, and others probably took service with King Agis of Sparta, who was not committed to the support of Alexander's 'Pan-Hellenic' war. Several high-ranking Persians, more resolute than Darius himself, were killed in the battle. Some of these had been survivors from the Granicus.

Considering the decisive nature of Alexander's victory, the actual duration of the fighting, for all its violence, must have been remarkably short. The battle was fought on a November day, yet there seems to have remained daylight enough for a long and eventful pursuit of the defeated army. In the morning, Alexander had advanced deliberately and slowly towards the Persian positions, and there had been time for both sides to observe each other and re-order their battle lines accordingly. The time taken by the battle itself cannot have been more than a few hours.

Arrian, despite his mention of phalanx casualties, gives no comprehensive figures of Macedonian losses. Other writers are in agreement with Arrian and with each other on the numbers of Persian dead but differ in their report of Alexander's casualties. It would seem, however, that the victorious army lost no more than a few hundred dead.

AFTER ISSUS

On the death of Memnon, the Persian admirals Pharnabazus and Autophradates had taken over command of Darius's Aegean fleet and continued to base themselves at Chios. They also continued to implement Memnon's strategy, which had been to erode Macedonian power in the Greek mainland and islands while Alexander was occupied with a career of eastward conquest.

Meanwhile in Greece, Agis, King of Sparta, a state that had never acknowledged Macedonian leadership, was thinking on the same lines as the Persians and hoped to concert his efforts with theirs. He sailed with a single trireme to meet Pharnabazus on the island of Siphnos in the Cyclades, his objective being to obtain a subsidy of ships and money from the Persians in support of a war against Antipater, Alexander's viceroy in Greece.

The news of Issus reached Agis and the Persian commanders precisely as they were conferring in Siphnos. Pharnabazus hastened back to Chios. Indeed, there was a danger that all along the east Aegean seaboard pro-Macedonian elements might take heart at Alexander's victory and throw off Persian control. In the circumstances, Agis certainly did not receive the contribution he had hoped for: Autophradates gave him just ten ships and thirty talents of silver. These he sent to his brother Agesilaus, with instructions that the rowers should be paid in full and the flotilla dispatched to Crete, there to establish an anti-Macedonian presence. This operation was successfully carried out.

Some months later, Agis was joined by Greek mercenaries who had opposed Alexander at Issus but escaped after the battle. (The number of the original fugitives is reported as 8,000; some returned to Greece via Egypt and some may have remained in that country.) Agis received no support from Athens. In the Peloponnese, several cities rallied to the Spartan call, but Messene, Argos and Megalopolis – all Sparta's traditional enemies – were in no mind to oppose the Macedonians. Agis's problem was thus one of numbers, and when he was at last confronted before the walls of a hostile Megalopolis by Antipater's Macedonian relief force, he was overwhelmed by an army twice as large as his own. He himself died heroically, still fighting on his knees when a leg wound made it impossible for him to stand.

At sea, on the other hand, the Persians enjoyed the numerical advantage, having even recruited many pirate crews into their fleet. But this, as events turned out, did not enable them to dislodge the Macedonians. In attempts to guard and threaten various points in the Aegean simul-

▶ *This clear copy from the relief at Persepolis shows the spherical butt-weight on a Persian spear. Persian troops who carried spears of this kind were sometimes known as 'apple-bearers' ('melophoroi' in Greek). Herodotus, writing of Xerxes' invasion of Greece, mentions the King's élite infantry as having spear butts in the form of gold and silver pomegranates and apples. Gold evidently ranked higher than silver, and apples ranked higher than pomegranates. Darius III at Gaugamela was followed by an élite of 'apple-bearers'.*

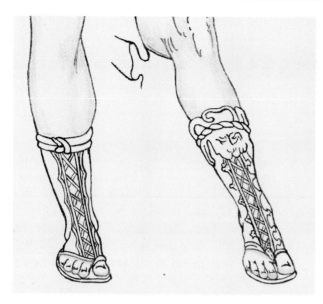

▲The 'cothurnus' (kothornos), of which two examples are shown here, was something between a boot and a legging, which left the toes exposed. It was worn by horsemen and, in an age like Alexander's when neither stirrups nor spurs were in use, it must have been welcome as providing extra grip on a horse's flanks. A man who could afford a horse was normally richer than one who could not, and possibly for this reason the 'cothurnus' acquired a certain social prestige. Persons of rank and consequence were often portrayed wearing it, as were gods and goddesses.

taneously, they split their forces too often. Units of the Persian navy that tried to recover command of the Hellespont were defeated by Alexander's fleet under the Macedonian officers Hegelochus and Amphoterus. Miletus was retaken by the Macedonians, and Pharnabazus himself was captured at Chios. The pirate crews the Persians had enlisted were arrested and executed.

At about the same time, there was some revival of the Persian war effort in the interior of Asia Minor. Darius's officers in Paphlagonia and Cappadocia managed to raise local levies from these provinces, and they were joined by fugitives from Issus, many of whom, despite the heavy Persian casualties in the battle, had made their way northward. These forces now threatened Antigonus, the commander to whom Alexander had entrusted Phrygia. Antigonus was all the more vulnerable because he had drafted troops to support Alexander's own operations farther east, and the Phrygian garrison forces were now de-

pleted. However, when the clash came, Antigonus vanquished the newly constituted Persian army in three separate engagements. Again, there was proof that Alexander had chosen the right man to fight the wars he left in his wake, and he himself was never obliged to deviate from his original plan as he led his forces southwards through Syria and Palestine.

At Damascus, Alexander captured a number of noble Persian ladies, of the families of Darius's officers who had been quartered there before the battle. He treated them with scrupulous detachment – with only one exception. Barsinē, the widow of Memnon, herself the daughter of a Persian nobleman, became his mistress, and she later bore him a son, whom he called Heracles in honour of his boasted ancestor.

Darius, when he had reached the other side of the Euphrates and recovered from his precipitate flight, sent a letter to Alexander offering peace on terms that in the circumstances could not be other than conciliatory. Alexander received the offer while encamped near Aradus on the Syrian coast, an island city which had received him with friendship, although its king was absent serving with the Persian Aegean fleet. In his letter, Darius reproached Alexander with an act of unprovoked aggression, but now offered friendship in return for the restoration of his wife, mother and daughters. To this, Alexander replied haughtily. Historical pretexts apart, he repudiated the charge of unprovoked aggression, accusing Darius of having aided the enemies of Macedon among the Greek cities and of having plotted King Philip's murder. In any case, he rejected all question of a negotiated peace, demanding nothing less than unconditional surrender. In fact, the tone of the letter was such that no surrender seemed to satisfy him – it was a challenge to Darius to continue fighting.

Alexander obviously preferred war to any peace. Perhaps his whole career should be regarded as a variation on the time-honoured policy of waging war abroad to preserve peace at home. However, in Alexander's favour it must be urged that he did not merely preserve peace in Greece. He imposed it where it had never previously existed.

THE SIEGE OF TYRE

Having been accepted by other Phoenician cities, Alexander hoped to receive the submission of Tyre without bloodshed. The King of Tyre, like the King of Aradus, was away serving with the Persian Aegean fleet, but Tyrian envoys met him at his approach to the city and assured him in general terms that the city rulers were ready to place themselves at his disposal. However, he put their goodwill to the test by expressing his wish to sacrifice at the shrine of Heracles inside the city; for the Tyrians recognized a Phoenician god who was identified by the Greeks as Heracles, and from this deity Alexander claimed descent. Tyrian goodwill unfortunately did not extend so far as to grant him the permission he sought. While the issue between the kings of Macedon and Persia was still undecided, they could not be expected to take sides with one or the other. In short, they would not admit him into the city.

The whole purpose of Alexander's present campaign was to leave no possible Persian base in his rear before marching eastward to resume hostilities with Darius himself. He could make no exceptions, especially in the case of a powerful naval centre like Tyre. The defences of the city appeared impregnable, but Alexander already seems to have regarded himself as invincible and was certainly so considered by the men who followed him. The siege of Tyre began.

So lengthy and laborious an operation is

▲ This illustration is taken from a Greek vase found in Italy. The vase dates from about 500BC, the date at which Miletus and other Greek cities of Asia Minor rose in revolt againt the Persian King Darius I. The revolt led to the Persian invasion of Greece, which Alexander claimed to avenge by his offensive on the Persian mainland a century and a half later. The warship shown here is moving under sail and oar. At this date, sails were usually left ashore when ships went into action. The carefully calculated manoeuvres that made possible the use of their rams depended on the unhampered skill of the rowers. In the illustration, the bronze ram can be seen, fashioned in the shape of a boar's head, at water level, beyond the prow.

Tyre: The Attack on Alexander's Mole

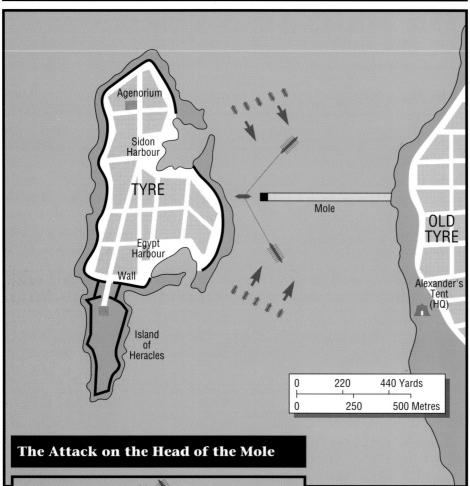

The Attack on the Head of the Mole

◄Note that offshore Tyre originally comprised two islands, which were united artificially in the 10th century BC. The wall that defended the northern island in its southern sector was probably still retained as an inner fortification in Alexander's day. The whole coastline here has silted up considerably since then, joining the island to the mainland.

◄When the fire-ship had been grounded according to plan and set alight the towers, the triremes that had towed it lay close to the mole and attacked Alexander's firefighters with missiles. As soon as the towers were on fire other Tyrians sallied out in boats and destroyed the palisades on the mole.

▲This drawing is from a Greek coin of Asia Minor dated about 300BC. It thus illustrates a type of ship probably in service in Alexander's lifetime. The ram, as frequently in later illustrations of ancient warships, is three-pronged, replacing the earlier boar's-head or single-pronged design. The forecastle seems to enclose a cabin and also supports an upper deck, which extends the full length of the hull.

appropriately termed a siege, though from the first Alexander's purpose was to storm rather than starve the city into surrender. In these waters, the Phoenician fleets, which served the Persians, were still supreme, and the island of Tyre could easily be supplied and supported from the sea. Alexander therefore decided to build a mole from the mainland to the island across the narrow water that separated them, a distance of about half a mile.

The building of Alexander's causeway at first proceeded briskly. The water near the mainland was shallow and the bottom muddy, and building material in the form of rock and timber was easily obtainable. Stakes were soon driven into the mud, which also made good binding material for the stone blocks above. But farther out the sea became suddenly deep, and close to the island it reached

a depth of three fathoms. The builders' task here became both difficult and dangerous: not only had they to contend with the deep water, but they were within missile range of the city walls. Furthermore, the Tyrians were able to row their galleys in from the sea and harass the builders, making work practically impossible.

To these tactics Alexander replied by building two towers upon the mole, covering their wooden structures with hides to give protection against missiles and render the wood less vulnerable to incendiary attack. He mounted artillery catapults in the towers and was thus able to retaliate against the raids of enemy ships by counterblasts of heavy missiles. The Tyrians then realized that they must at all cost destroy the towers, and they resorted to the use of a fire-ship. They made ready a

Tyre: Alexander's Blockade

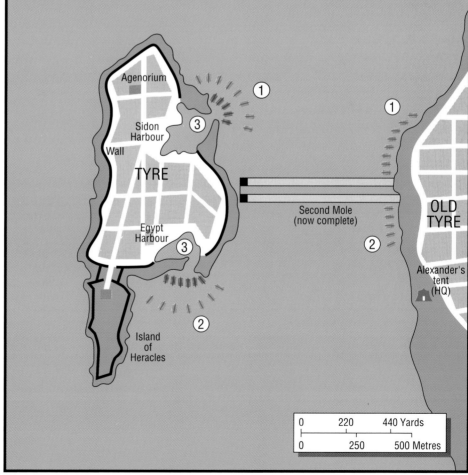

▶
1. 120 Cyprian ships under Andromachus.

2. 80 Phoenician ships plus 23 from Rhodes, Lycia, Soli and Mallus, and one Macedonian penteconter.

3. Tyrian ships.

capacious vessel, which had been a horse transport, filling it with wood shavings, chips, pitch, sulphur and every combustible material that they could lay hands on. Double yard-arms were fixed to the masts, and on these were hung cauldrons of oily substances that could be relied upon to feed the flames. The fire-ship was also ballasted at the stern end in such a way as to tilt the prow upward over the edge of the mole and close to the foot of the towers. It was then towed in by triremes, and the crew that had manned the old hulk easily swam away when she was alight.

The result was what had been hoped – the towers were soon ablaze. Other Tyrian galleys cruised inshore, close to the mole, and put down a barrage of missiles, which prevented Alexander's fire-fighters approaching the towers. A sally was also launched from the city in small boats. Temporary landings were made on the mole, and its defensive palisades were torn down. Artillery catapults that had escaped the havoc wrought by the fire-ship were additionally set on fire by the daring raiders.

This obviously was a great setback to Alexander. But as a strategist he possessed an indefatigable patience, which contrasted strangely with the fierce impetuosity of his tactics in battle. He now gave orders that the mole should be widened to accommodate a greater number of towers. More artillery catapults were also to be constructed. While the work was being carried out, he took with him a contingent of hypaspists and Agrianian light troops and marched back to revisit the friendly Phoenicians of Sidon, where he had left his own

▲ This coin, with its representation of an anchor, dates from about 350BC – in Alexander's lifetime. Unlike some other examples of ancient anchors, it has a stock. It is tempting to attribute the broad fin-like arms of the anchor to the artist's ignorance or want of skill, but maximum weight with minimum stowage space was always a prime consideration, and various designs must have been used in order to achieve it. When Alexander anchored his siege ships under the walls of Tyre, they perhaps relied on anchors of this type.

triremes. A navy he must have: for without superiority at sea, Tyre could not be captured.

Meanwhile, the naval commanders of the Phoenician cities of Aradus and Byblus, impressed by Alexander's victory at Issus, abandoned the Persian admiral Autophradates, with whose fleet they had been serving, and deserted to Alexander. Ten triremes also came over to him from Rhodes. Another thirteen such vessels joined him from the cities of the Lycian and Cilician coasts, and a fifty-oared galley came from Macedon itself. The massive desertion of the Phoenicians, with 80 ships, had its repercussions in Cyprus, whose kings were also anxious to be on the winning side. A combined Cyprian fleet of 120 ships soon sailed to Sidon and swelled Alexander's already growing navy as it lay there in readiness.

He may be considered to have enjoyed a great stroke of good fortune, for the naval windfall came to him just at the time when he most needed it. On the other hand, the event may be regarded as a merited psychological product of his own resounding victory at Issus. He was in any case glad to overlook his new allies' earlier hostility to him, treating their previous adherence to the Persian cause as a case of *force majeure*.

Naval Operations

While the construction of his artillery engines was being completed, Alexander made a foray into Arabian territory inland, and after a ten-day demonstration of strength, in which he used a few cavalry squadrons with hypaspists and Agrianes, he received the submission of the people in this area. He perhaps regarded the raid as a military training exercise, but in any case it fitted well with his general strategy of leaving no active enemy in his rear.

On his return from this expedition, he found that Cleander, the son of Polemocrates, whom he had sent to Greece to recruit mercenaries, had returned with a body of 4,000 Peloponnesian troops. He was thus well prepared for a new confrontation with the Tyrians. As regards naval strength, he had certainly turned the tables on them; nor did they realize until he was ready for battle that his fleet had been dramatically increased by the Phoenician and Cyprian contingents.

Leading his fleet from a warship on the right wing, he had hoped at first to tempt the Tyrians to a naval engagement in the open sea. He had posted marines on the decks of his galleys and he was prepared either for boarding or ramming tactics. However, when they recognized the superiority of the numbers ranged against them the Tyrians prudently avoided this and concentrated merely on holding the entrance of their harbours in the face of the oncoming enemy; any fighting would then be in narrow waters, where Alexander's numbers could not be deployed to advantage.

The two harbours of the island faced north and south respectively, one towards Sidon, the other towards Egypt. Seeing their entrances heavily defended, Alexander did not at once try to force an entry. The mouth of the north harbour, as he approached, was blocked by triremes moored bow-on to him. But his Phoenician galleys sank three of the enemy ships that were anchored in a slightly exposed position, ramming them head-on. The crews escaped easily enough, swimming back on to the friendly territory of the island.

After this brief encounter, Alexander berthed his ships along the mainland shore and encamped on the adjacent land at a point where the mole gave some protection from the weather. His own headquarters were southwards, looking towards the island's southern harbour. He ordered the Cyprian fleet to blockade the north side of the island and the Phoenicians the south.

He had meanwhile recruited a large number of artificers both from Cyprus and the Phoenician coast. The construction of siege engines had proceeded swiftly, and these were installed on the extremity of the mole as well as on the besieging ships, both transports and slow triremes, which Alexander had caused to be anchored all around the city preparatory to bombarding the high walls. (These walls are reported as being 150 feet high on the side facing the mole. Even assuming that this refers to the height of the towers rather than the curtain wall, the figure seems exaggerated; the Mausoleum at Halicarnassus, one of the seven wonders of the ancient world, was only 134 feet

high.) The masonry opposite the mole was massive, consisting of large mortared stone blocks. On top of these, the Tyrians now built wooden towers in order that they might increase their advantage of height, and they showered down missiles of every kind, including fire-darts, on the besieging ships. As a further device, they piled rocks in the sea under their walls, and this kept Alexander's vessels at a distance. As far as possible, Alexander hauled away the rocks, but this work had to be carried on from ships anchored nearby. The Tyrians accordingly armour-plated some of their triremes and ran in against the anchored siege vessels, cutting their moorings. Alexander retaliated by armouring some of his own light (thirty-oared) ships and obstructing the enemy triremes. The Tyrians then sent down divers to cut the mooring cables, but Alexander replaced these mooring ropes with chains, which could not be cut. On the landward side, his men also managed to throw out ropes from the mole and noose some of the rocks that had been dumped on the sea-bed. These rocks were then winched out and slung into deep water, where they created no difficulty or danger. The approach to the wall was thus at last clear, and Alexander's ships were able to lie under it unmolested.

The Tyrians, now increasingly conscious of their danger, realized that they must challenge the blockading navy in some action at sea, and they decided to attack the Cyprian contingent, choosing the hour of the midday heat when the vigilance of the besiegers was relaxed and Alexander himself had retired to his tent to rest.

For this purpose they manned three quinqueremes, three quadriremes and seven triremes with picked crews and the best-armed fighting complements they could muster. The sails of the Tyrian ships in the harbour were used to screen their preparations, and the men went aboard unobserved by enemy watchers at sea or on land. The Tyrian flotilla now glided out of the north harbour in line ahead and at an angle where it was still unperceived by the enemy. On board, dead silence was maintained – even the boatswains did not call the stroke to the rowers. Only when they came within sight of the Cyprians did they permit themselves the ordinary words of command and

The Tyrian Sally

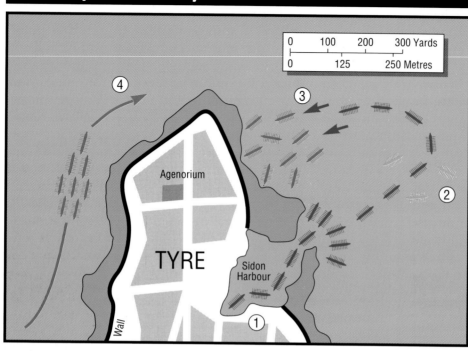

◄ *Midday: Alexander's ships at anchor and almost unmanned.*

1. Tyrian galleys screened by ships in the harbour mouth.

2. 3 Cyprian ships sunk.

3. Other Cyprian ships driven ashore for breaking up.

4: Approach of Alexander. The Tyrian ships raced for safety but were mostly rammed by Alexander's flotilla (5 triremes and a few quinqueremes) before they could reach harbour. Tyrian crews saved themselves by swimming.

break out into battle-cries. They then achieved a formidable surprise attack. At the first onslaught, they rammed and sank the quinqueremes of the Cyprian King Pnytagoras, as well as those of Androcles and Pasicrates – from the Cypriot cities of Amathus and Curion respectively. Other Cyprian ships were forced ashore and broken up. Indeed, the attack had been made when most of the anchored Cyprian fleet was unmanned.

However, the Tyrians were not entirely fortunate. It so happened that on this day Alexander had not taken his usual siesta but returned almost immediately to the ships. Quickly aware of the enemy sally, he reacted at once and ordered men aboard. The first ships that were manned were commanded to block the southern harbour mouth and to ensure that no further sortie was made from that quarter. He then put out with a few quinqueremes and some five triremes and sailed around the city to challenge those of the enemy who had already broken out.

The Tyrian watchers on the battlements, observing Alexander's moves, tried to warn their comrades on the sea and nearby shore, but the seamen were deafened by the din of their own

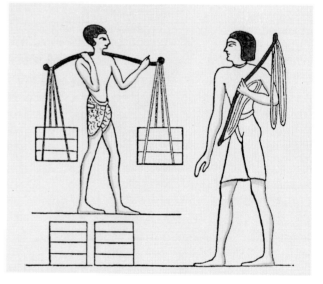

▲ *This picture from an Egyptian tomb shows a slave carrying bricks made of Nile mud. In early centuries, city walls were often built of such bricks, but by Alexander's time masonry defences were common. Developments in siege warfare necessitated stronger* fortifications. *Alexander found the walls at Tyre on the landward side constructed from mortared stone blocks, but on the southern seaward sector, where he ultimately breached a weak spot, softer material may have been used.*

THE SIEGE OF TYRE

wrecking operations. When they understood what was happening it was too late – only a few of their ships made it back to harbour in time. The majority were rammed and disabled. A quinquereme and quadrireme were captured by Alexander's men. Human casualties, however, were not many. For the Tyrian crews, as often happened in ancient sea fights, saved themselves by swimming.

The Breaching of the Wall

The walls of Tyre were now closely beset, and even the defenders' sally had been a costly and limited success. The walls themselves, however, still presented a formidable obstacle. In the north, the Greek contingent towed up siege engines, but the solidity of the walls defied their efforts. In the south, a part of the wall was slightly shaken, and a small breach was made, into which gangways were tentatively thrown. But the Macedonian assault party that tried to use the gangways was easily repulsed by the Tyrians.

After a three-day interval, however, with calmer weather prevailing, more siege engines were towed up to the same spot, and the breach was enlarged. Two ships carrying gangways then approached, under command of Admetus and Coenus respectively, and the way was open for a fresh assault. This was led by Alexander's best troops. The hypaspists were commanded by Admetus, who distinguished himself by valour in the ensuing action. The Foot Companions were led by Coenus, who in the future was to prove one

▶ *The final assault on Tyre:*

1. Alexander's second mole completed. Siege engines made no impression on such strong defences.

2. Siege engines mounted on ships.

3. Harbour mouths defended by Tyrian ships and blockaded by Alexander's fleet (Phoenicians in the south, Cyprians in the north).

4. Diversionary tactics. Ships were beached under the walls for battering operations, or lay close and launched missiles.

5. Probing attacks.

6. Eventual breach (approximate position).

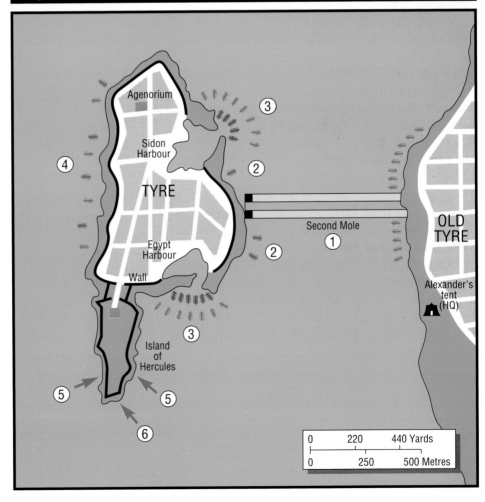

Tyre: 'The Weak Spot'

of Alexander's most trusted commanders.

At the same time, widespread diversions and feints were made all round the perimeter of the city, as the besieging ships everywhere moved close under the walls. Attempts were already being made to penetrate the two harbours. The sector of the wall where Alexander himself was taking part in the assault was the first to be captured, Admetus being the first man upon the ramparts. Some of the towers that crowned the battlements were now occupied, and this gave the Macedonians control of the linking curtain walls. Soon Alexander's men were fighting their way down into the city itself.

Even when the Tyrians had been driven from the walls, they defended the Agenorium at the north end of the city – a citadel named after Tyre's legendary King Agenor. Many of the defenders died fighting where they stood. Others were dispersed by Alexander and his hypaspists. The city was now entered from the harbours as well as from the walls. Alexander's Phoenician fleet broke the boom in the south and destroyed the shipping it had sheltered. In the north there was no boom and the Cyprians met little resistance when they sailed in. As Coenus' troops entered, the city was a scene of bloody massacre. The Macedonians were embittered by the length of the siege, and also by an incident in which the Tyrians had killed prisoners upon the walls before the eyes of the besiegers.

8,000 Tyrians were killed. Of Alexander's forces, up to 400 Macedonians are reported as having lost their lives in the siege; of these, 20 were hypaspists who fell with the heroic Admetus in the final assault. In the city at the time of its capture were many Carthaginian pilgrims, who had visited their mother city, according to custom, to pay honour to Melcart, the Phoenician Heracles – in whose temple they now took refuge. These Alexander spared. But other foreigners, together with Tyrian survivors, were sold into slavery – about 30,000 persons in all.

Alexander sacrificed to Heracles in fulfilment of his original avowed intent. The god's complacency over the treatment of a city where he had received supreme honour seems to have been easily assumed. The entire siege had taken seven months, from January to July 332BC.

Egyptian Interlude

Even before Tyre was taken, Alexander had received a further letter from Darius. The Persian king proposed 10,000 talents ransom for the captured ladies of his family and offered Alexander all Persian territory west of the Euphrates, together with the hand of his daughter in marriage. Alexander replied that he already possessed and controlled the territory in question and that he was free to marry Darius's daughter with or without her father's consent. If Darius had any favours to ask, he should come to Alexander and sue for them in person.

Alexander now marched for Egypt in pursuit of his immediate strategic objective, which was to secure the whole of the eastern Mediterranean coastline. No city dared resist him, with the single exception of Gaza. This stronghold was defended as fanatically as Tyre had been: its Phoenician ruler recruited into his service large numbers of Arab mercenaries and laid in considerable stores and provisions. Unlike Tyre, however, Gaza was not an island. Alexander surrounded the city walls with an earthwork of his own. After sallies and counter-sallies, he was able to sap the wall towers and bring up ladders against the battered fortifications. When Gaza was finally taken, most of its male population died fighting; women and children were sold into slavery.

With the example of Tyre and Gaza before them, the Egyptians were in no mind to oppose Alexander. In any case, Egypt was not a province like other parts of the Persian Empire. It had been conquered in 525BC by the Persian King Cambyses. The successful resistance of the Greeks to Persian invasions in 490 and 480BC had shown that the Persians were not invincible, and Egypt had been restless and rebellious throughout much of the fifth century, regaining independence in 404BC. Only a few years before Alexander's arrival had it been reconquered for Persia. Sabaces, the Persian governor of Egypt, had in fact been killed at Issus, and his successor accepted Alexander without demur.

The Egyptians regarded the Macedonian king as a liberator, and he in turn flattered Egyptian national sentiment, doing conspicuous honour to

▶ *Philip, Alexander's father, was an important pioneer in the use of catapult artillery in Greece. The illustration here shows a mechanical stone-thrower ('lithobolos') – a giant sling mounted on a heavy wooden frame. It is likely that both this and the dart-shooting catapult were well developed before Alexander embarked on the siege of Tyre and that he used both sling and crossbow types.*

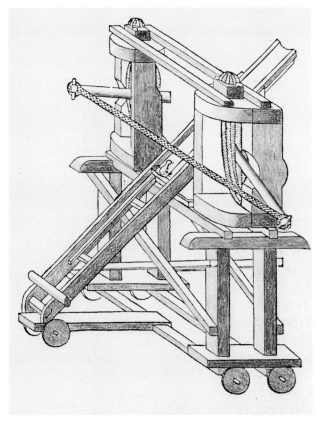

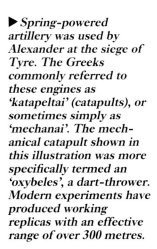

▲ *This sling-type catapult has no wheels but would have been adequate in sieges. More mobile catapults were developed in later centuries, though Alexander is reported as having used artillery machines in field operations. A dart-shooting catapult, mounted on its base, stood three or four foot high. Sling types were larger and more powerful but must have been less accurate.*

▶ *Spring-powered artillery was used by Alexander at the siege of Tyre. The Greeks commonly referred to these engines as 'katapeltai' (catapults), or sometimes simply as 'mechanai'. The mechanical catapult shown in this illustration was more specifically termed an 'oxybeles', a dart-thrower. Modern experiments have produced working replicas with an effective range of over 300 metres.*

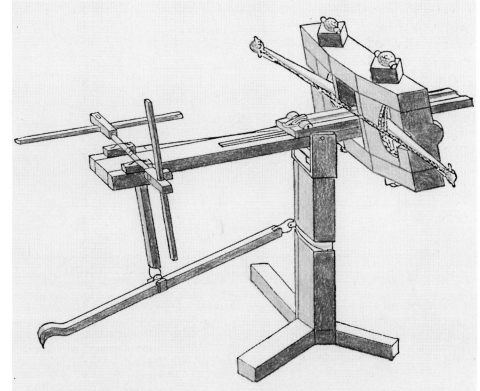

THE FALL OF TYRE

The final assault on the city, July 332BC

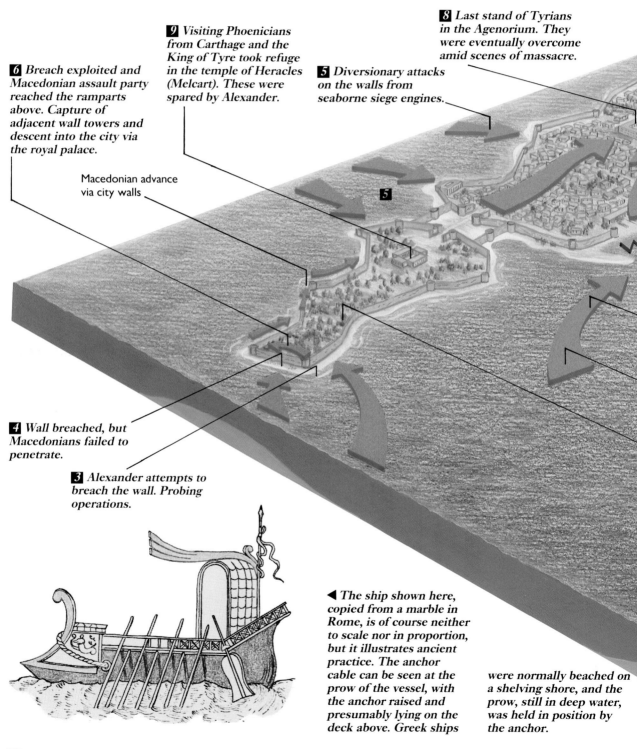

8 *Last stand of Tyrians in the Agenorium. They were eventually overcome amid scenes of massacre.*

9 *Visiting Phoenicians from Carthage and the King of Tyre took refuge in the temple of Heracles (Melcart). These were spared by Alexander.*

5 *Diversionary attacks on the walls from seaborne siege engines.*

6 *Breach exploited and Macedonian assault party reached the ramparts above. Capture of adjacent wall towers and descent into the city via the royal palace.*

Macedonian advance via city walls

4 *Wall breached, but Macedonians failed to penetrate.*

3 *Alexander attempts to breach the wall. Probing operations.*

◀ *The ship shown here, copied from a marble in Rome, is of course neither to scale nor in proportion, but it illustrates ancient practice. The anchor cable can be seen at the prow of the vessel, with the anchor raised and presumably lying on the deck above. Greek ships were normally beached on a shelving shore, and the prow, still in deep water, was held in position by the anchor.*

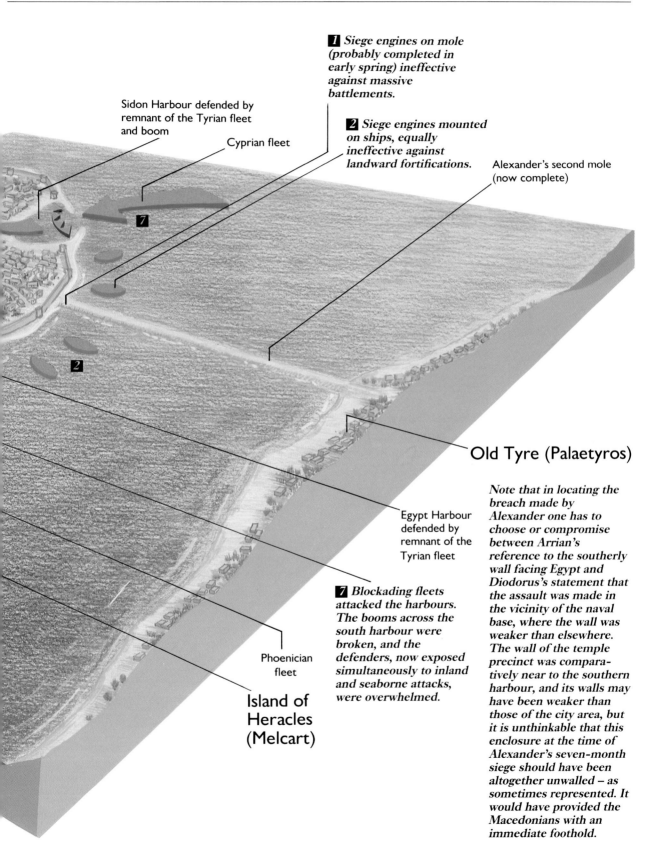

1 *Siege engines on mole (probably completed in early spring) ineffective against massive battlements.*

2 *Siege engines mounted on ships, equally ineffective against landward fortifications.*

Alexander's second mole (now complete)

Sidon Harbour defended by remnant of the Tyrian fleet and boom

Cyprian fleet

Old Tyre (Palaetyros)

Egypt Harbour defended by remnant of the Tyrian fleet

7 *Blockading fleets attacked the harbours. The booms across the south harbour were broken, and the defenders, now exposed simultaneously to inland and seaborne attacks, were overwhelmed.*

Phoenician fleet

Island of Heracles (Melcart)

Note that in locating the breach made by Alexander one has to choose or compromise between Arrian's reference to the southerly wall facing Egypt and Diodorus's statement that the assault was made in the vicinity of the naval base, where the wall was weaker than elsewhere. The wall of the temple precinct was compara-tively near to the southern harbour, and its walls may have been weaker than those of the city area, but it is unthinkable that this enclosure at the time of Alexander's seven-month siege should have been altogether unwalled – as sometimes represented. It would have provided the Macedonians with an immediate foothold.

their gods. Alexander took over the official treasury from Mazaces, the new governor, and garrisoned Pelusium at the eastern extremity of the Nile delta. He made a round tour over the desert via Heliopolis and Memphis, the ancient Egyptian capital and religious shrine, returning down the Nile to its mouth north of Mareotis.

It is not always possible to find a purely military motive for Alexander's movements. From Egypt he marched across the desert to visit the oracle of Ammon at the Libyan oasis of Siwa. Either piety or curiosity or a mixture of both may have prompted him. Command of a conquering army in any case made for convenient travelling. At Siwa, the oracle was said to have hailed Alexander as son of Zeus – with whom the Egyptian deity Ammon was identified. Perhaps Alexander interpreted too literally what was merely a courteous form of address, but he was never reluctant to accept divine honours.

On return to Memphis, he reorganized the political administration of Egypt, replacing Persian officials with Egyptians, but he left the garrisons of Pelusium and Memphis under command of his own officers. Modest reinforcements meanwhile reached him from the Aegean area: 400 Greek mercenaries sent by Antipater and 500 Thracian cavalry. Hegelochus, Alexander's victorious commander in the north-east Aegean, had also arrived in Egypt, bringing with him prisoners; but Pharnabazus, the Persian admiral captured in Chios, had escaped.

Usually, the men whom Alexander left in control of his military administration were well chosen. There were, however, inevitable exceptions. In charge of his military treasure chest, he retained a civilian official named Harpalus. This man, among others, had taken Alexander's side in the course of domestic quarrels and palace intrigues during Philip's lifetime, and among others he had suffered exile as a result. Alexander, on accession to the throne, had recalled the exiles and rewarded them with positions of trust – a trust of which this man at least was to prove unworthy. Harpalus admittedly did not remain in Egypt but served with the army as paymaster, when previous paymasters had been appointed to the Egyptian Treasury. However, the time was to come when

Harpalus was again in a position to abuse his office and this he did.

Alexander had now completed the first phase of his grand strategy. He had firmly secured the whole of the east Mediterranean seaboard, and in summer 331 he again marched eastward in pursuit of Darius, reaching Thapsacus on the Euphrates in August. Darius's forces, under his officer Mazaeus, had held the crossing of the Euphrates against the Macedonian advance guard, but they fled on news that Alexander himself was approaching. Indeed, numbering 3,000 cavalry in all, they could not prudently have done otherwise.

After crossing the Euphrates, Alexander did not march directly on Babylon, which might have seemed his next most obvious target, but turned northwards, hugging the foothills of the Armenian mountains, where foraging was easier and the heat less oppressive. But he probably already suspected – as his scouts soon confirmed – that Darius was waiting for him on the farther side of the Tigris, ready to fall upon his rear if he turned southwards. At the same time, from the intelligence he had gained, it appeared that the Persians intended to block his passage if he attempted to cross the river. In fact, at the higher point where he ultimately crossed, the Tigris was undefended. That did not mean the crossing was easy, for his men were in danger of being swept away by the rapidity of the current, and they needed a good rest after the obstacle had been overcome.

Nor was the Tigris the only natural hazard to face Alexander at this time. An eclipse of the moon provoked throes of agonized superstition among his soldiers, which could have ended in a mutiny. But the Egyptian seers whom he had taken with him on his eastward march, out of respect for their lore and learning, served him well: they realized perfectly that lunar eclipses are caused by regular movements of the sun, moon and earth. However, their knowledge of astronomy was supplemented by an at least equal knowledge of human nature. Instead of trying to explain the movements of the heavenly bodies, they declared the eclipse to be a *good* omen signifying Alexander's victory in the near future. The army was at once reassured, and here at least was proof that the Egyptians sincerely supported the Macedonian cause!

THE BATTLE OF GAUGAMELA

Four days after crossing the River Tigris, Alexander's scouts sighted Persian cavalry in the distance. On being informed, Alexander drew up his army in order of battle and, thus deployed, advanced slowly. Later intelligence revealed that the Persian force was but an advance party, no more than 1,000 in number. Leaving his army to continue its slow advance, Alexander rode on ahead with his royal squadron and a detachment of light Paeonian horsemen. The Persians fled at his approach, but he gave chase, killing some of the enemy and capturing others. From these prisoners he learned much concerning the strength and movements of Darius's army and of the various contingents that formed it. The Persian Empire, even after Alexander had detached from it Asia Minor, Egypt and the Levant coast, was still vast, and its military potential was formidable.

The Advance to Gaugamela

Bessus, satrap of Bactria, in the north-easterly Persian dominions (corresponding to modern north Afghanistan and adjacent territories) led an army from this region, which also included a unit of Indians. Other contingents were of Asiatic Scythians, Arachotians (from southern Afghanistan), Hyrcanians from south of the Caspian and their eastern neighbours the Areians under the satrap Satibarzanes. Also recruited were Persian Gulf tribesmen, Medes and associated peoples, forces drawn from the regions of Susa and Babylon, with Mesopotamian Syrians under Darius's trusted commander, Mazaeus. The total numbers reported amounted to 40,000 cavalry, 1,000,000 infantry, 200 scythe-wheeled chariots, and a few elephants, perhaps fifteen in number, contributed by Indians from west of the Indus.

This army had encamped near Gaugamela (literally: 'The Camel's House'), a village beside the River Bumodus 75 miles west of Arbela. Recognizing his fault at Issus, Darius had chosen a wide plain for his battlefield, where cavalry could be deployed and chariots used to advantage. The Persian King had even given orders that the ground in this area should be levelled where it was uneven in order to facilitate chariot tactics.

As soon as Alexander knew that Darius was

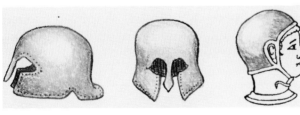

Simpler helmets are here placed beside more ornate types for the sake of contrast. The simpler but skilfully wrought Corinthian type (on left) had mainly been superseded by Alexander's time. The helmet known to archaeologists as the

'Thracian' type (bottom right), with its crellated cheek pieces and flowing crest, was more characteristic of the late fourth century BC. Our knowledge of highly decorated helmets is derived from ancient representations rather than surviving specimens.

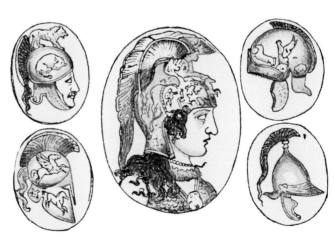

GAUGAMELA: THE OPENING MOVES

The advance to battle, 30 September to 1 October 331BC

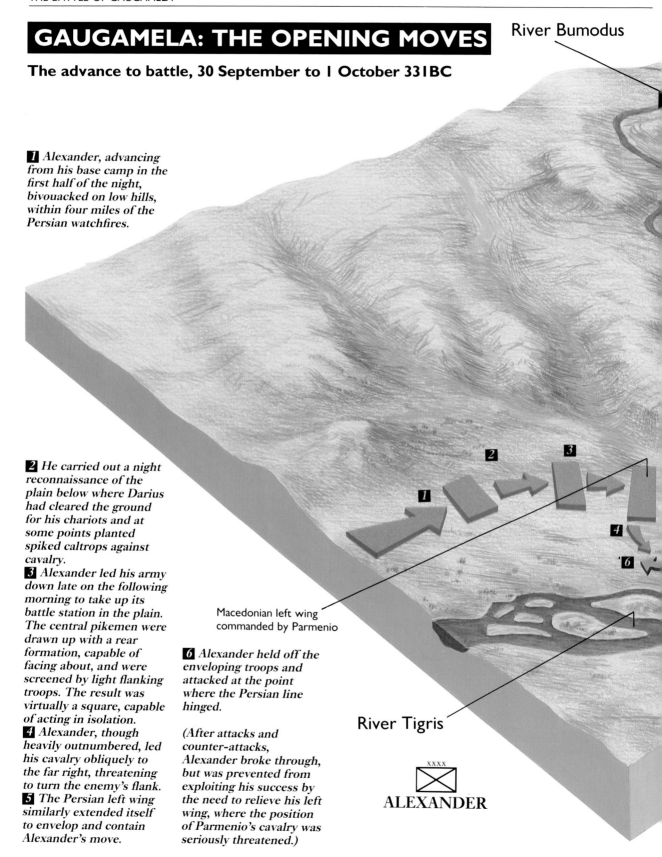

River Bumodus

1 Alexander, advancing from his base camp in the first half of the night, bivouacked on low hills, within four miles of the Persian watchfires.

2 He carried out a night reconnaissance of the plain below where Darius had cleared the ground for his chariots and at some points planted spiked caltrops against cavalry.

3 Alexander led his army down late on the following morning to take up its battle station in the plain. The central pikemen were drawn up with a rear formation, capable of facing about, and were screened by light flanking troops. The result was virtually a square, capable of acting in isolation.

4 Alexander, though heavily outnumbered, led his cavalry obliquely to the far right, threatening to turn the enemy's flank.

5 The Persian left wing similarly extended itself to envelop and contain Alexander's move.

Macedonian left wing commanded by Parmenio

6 Alexander held off the enveloping troops and attacked at the point where the Persian line hinged.

(After attacks and counter-attacks, Alexander broke through, but was prevented from exploiting his success by the need to relieve his left wing, where the position of Parmenio's cavalry was seriously threatened.)

River Tigris

XXXX

ALEXANDER

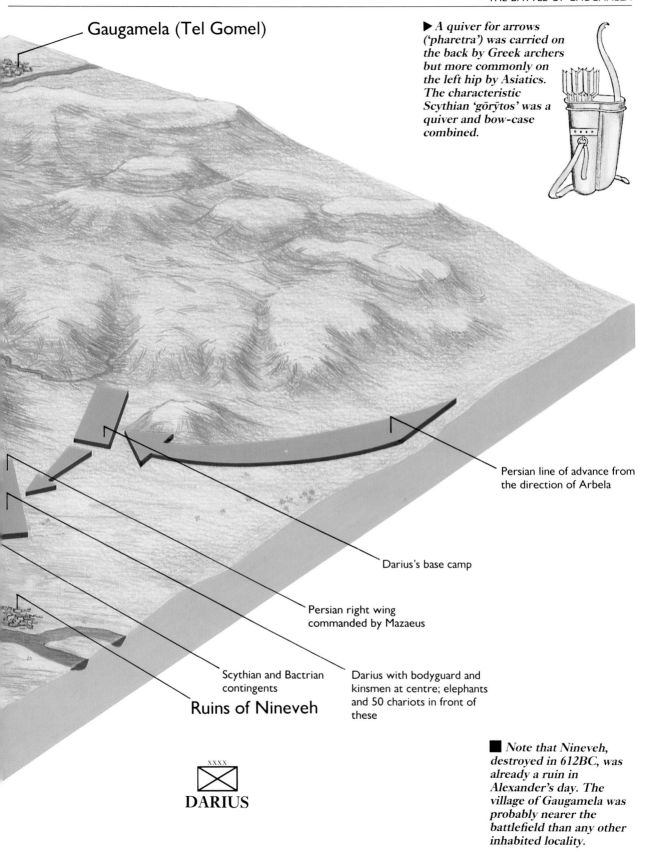

Gaugamela (Tel Gomel)

▶ *A quiver for arrows ('pharetra') was carried on the back by Greek archers but more commonly on the left hip by Asiatics. The characteristic Scythian 'gōrȳtos' was a quiver and bow-case combined.*

Persian line of advance from the direction of Arbela

Darius's base camp

Persian right wing commanded by Mazaeus

Scythian and Bactrian contingents

Darius with bodyguard and kinsmen at centre; elephants and 50 chariots in front of these

Ruins of Nineveh

XXXX
DARIUS

■ *Note that Nineveh, destroyed in 612BC, was already a ruin in Alexander's day. The village of Gaugamela was probably nearer the battlefield than any other inhabited locality.*

awaiting him, he halted his advance and made a camp, fortifying it with a ditch and stockade. Here he left all his baggage and pack animals, together with camp followers, non-combatant troops and prisoners, then by night led his fighting men forward, in battle order, with little equipment but their weapons. His purpose was to confront the enemy at dawn. The camps of the two armies were about seven miles apart. A range of hills still separated them, and they were not yet visible to each other.

Alexander had set off with his battle force about the second watch of the night (probably a few hours before midnight). After he had covered about half the distance between his camp and the enemy he found himself just over the crest of the intervening hills: here Persian positions were within view, vividly illuminated by their watch-fires.

The hills in which the Macedonians had halted must have been virtually treeless, and Alexander now deployed his army for battle. He held a council of war with his officers, and it was decided to bivouac where they were, still deployed in line of battle.

Taking with him a body of Companion cavalry and light-armed troops, Alexander rode down to reconnoitre Darius's chosen battlefield in the plain below. Moonlight must have enabled him to do this – indeed, moonlight in Middle Eastern countries can be very vivid. However, he must have kept his distance from the enemy lines, for it was no part of his plan to engage in night operations.

In fact, when he returned to the Macedonian positions, Parmenio is said to have suggested that he should make a night attack and so take the Persians off their guard. Alexander replied flippantly that it would be a pity to steal a victory in this way. He usually invited the opinions of his officers but took his own decisions without feeling obliged to account for them. Certainly, there were always incalculable factors in a night attack. It should also be noted in general that although Alexander often surprised his enemies by a rapid night march, he preferred to do his actual fighting in daylight.

The Persians, however, apparently feared that he would make such a night attack and, having built no camp, remained tediously throughout the hours of darkness drawn up under arms in their battle formations. The Macedonians, it is true, were also without a fortified camp in the position where they had halted. But the hillside offered a natural defence – certainly unnegotiable by Darius's chariot fleet – and they felt sufficiently secure to eat and rest.

The Persian battle order is known with some precision, for Darius's written instructions were afterwards captured. The left wing, facing Alexander himself on the Macedonian right, was held by Bactrian cavalry with Asiatic Scythians and

▼ *This illustration of a fallen warrior is based on a sculpture from Aegina. The greaves are seen in detail with close-fitting bands about the ankles. The illustration of a bronze shield and greaves represents objects found in an Etruscan tomb. They were probably imitated or purchased from Greek sources. The Macedonian phalangist, though in some respects more lightly armed than Greek hoplites, wore greaves. Like helmets, greaves, were lined with soft material to protect the wearer. 'Bronze shields' were usually formed from a wooden perishable core, but in some cases the bronze facings have survived.*

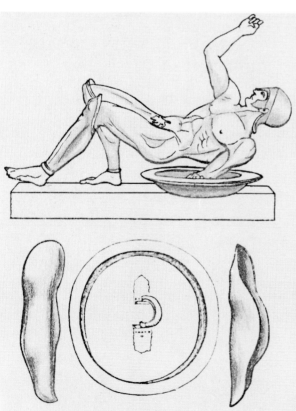

▶ The 'thorax' or corselet had in early Greek times been made of superimposed linen layers. Metal breast and back plates gave more protection but were, of course, heavier. By Alexander's epoch, elaborate composite corselets were manufactured by combining metal with perishable materials. Characteristic of most types were the shoulder pieces, which laced down over the chest.

▲ On the evidence of ancient vases and sculptures, Greek warriors and athletes normally went into action bare-footed. Bare feet allow the useful exercise of the toe muscles and give a good grip. However, it seems unlikely that Alexander led a bare-footed army to India and back. Xenophon's comrades in 400BC certainly wore some kind of laced footwear ('hypodemata'), when they marched from the Persian interior to the Black Sea. This illustration, from a British Museum marble, shows an ancient shoe with the wearer's toes, as normally, uncovered.

▶ The illustration is from an ancient cameo, representing the hero Achilles, to whom, as a Greek leader glorious in war against Asiatic enemies, Alexander paid special honour. Achilles' arms and armour as here depicted, however, are those of comparatively late historical times. The all-metal corselet is moulded to the shape of the body muscles, and this type is known to archaeologists as a 'muscle cuirasse'. The manner of slinging the sword from the shoulder on a baldric ('telamon') is clearly demonstrated. the Greek letters indicate the name of the engraver.

▲ A Persian cavalryman, based on a figure from the Issus mosaic, who may represent a Royal guard as he is shown fighting in defence of the Royal chariot. He is equipped with two cornel-wood javelins called palta; although no armour is visible, it is probable that he is wearing scale armour under his baggy tunic. Against Alexander's Macedonian cavalry the Persians seem to have thrown javelins and closed with hand weapons. Persian cavalry often suffered against their more heavily armoured Macedonian opponents. (Painting by Richard Geiger)

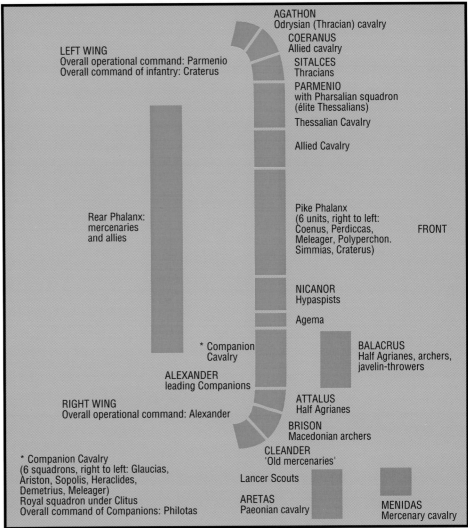

Battle of Gaugamela:
Alexander's Order of Battle and Battle Stations

AGATHON
Odrysian (Thracian) cavalry

COERANUS
Allied cavalry

SITALCES
Thracians

PARMENIO
with Pharsalian squadron
(élite Thessalians)

Thessalian Cavalry

Allied Cavalry

LEFT WING
Overall operational command: Parmenio
Overall command of infantry: Craterus

Rear Phalanx:
mercenaries
and allies

Pike Phalanx
(6 units, right to left:
Coenus, Perdiccas,
Meleager, Polyperchon.
Simmias, Craterus)

FRONT

NICANOR
Hypaspists

Agema

BALACRUS
Half Agrianes, archers,
javelin-throwers

* Companion
Cavalry

ALEXANDER
leading Companions

ATTALUS
Half Agrianes

RIGHT WING
Overall operational command: Alexander

BRISON
Macedonian archers

CLEANDER
'Old mercenaries'

Lancer Scouts

* Companion Cavalry
(6 squadrons, right to left: Glaucias,
Ariston, Sopolis, Heraclides,
Demetrius, Meleager)
Royal squadron under Clitus
Overall command of Companions: Philotas

ARETAS
Paeonian cavalry

MENIDAS
Mercenary cavalry

Phocion was a great Athenian statesman and soldier of Alexander's epoch. Unlike his political enemy Demosthenes, he stood for a sane and balanced attitude towards Macedon. In 318BC, the Athenians, adhering as often to the worst traditions of democracy, condemned Phocion to death. The illustration shows him wearing the kind of military cloak known as a 'chlamys'.

Arichotians. The Persians themselves were stationed in the centre. Here, in accordance with usual practice, the King with his royal entourage took up his position. The right wing was held by troops from Syria, Mesopotamia and the Persian Gulf. An advance force screened the left wing. This force was composed of Scythian cavalry, 1,000 Bactrians and 100 scythe-wheeled chariots. The elephants, with 50 chariots, were posted in front of Darius himself. Greek mercenaries, with Persian troops stationed on either side, were also drawn up in front of him in the central sector. These were the only forces that could be relied upon to face the Macedonian phalanx. Alexander's army numbered about 40,000 infantry and 7,000 cavalry.

Into Battle

In Greek and Macedonian battle tactics, there was always a tendency for the right wing of an army to outflank the enemy left. This was a natural consequence of the fact that spears were wielded in the right hand: the man on the extreme right edged outwards to gain additional elbow room and strike a more effective blow. Those who fought beside him on his left inevitably followed his outward move, to preserve their line intact and

prevent a gap developing, so that little by little, as each man closed up with his comrade on the right, there was a general drift in this direction. But though this led to the envelopment of the enemy left, there remained the danger that the enveloping force might lose contact with its own centre and leave a gap, which the enemy could easily exploit.

In Alexander's tactics, this danger became a calculated risk. He was always alert to the threats involved and took measures to offset them. In the first place, the right wing cavalry, which he commanded in person, was completely under his control and could be recalled, even in heady moments of victory and pursuit, to succour the hard-pressed central phalanx. Secondly, the phalanx was organized to some extent as a self-contained and self-reliant unit, maintaining its position and function at any rate until help could arrive.

▲ This illustration well illustrates the kind of lanyard that often ran round the interior of a concave Greek shield. A cord of this type could be used instead of a rigid hand grip ('antilabē'), and it also served for slinging the shield over the back during a march. The tasselled pegs were removable, and in a play of Aristophanes, the fact that they were in place was evidence that the shield was ready for immediate use.

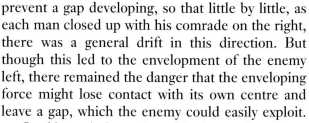

▼ Caltrops ('triboloi') were spikes so placed as to render ground impassable to cavalry. They were of two kinds: those planted in the soil and those simply strewn on the surface. The illustration shows an instance of the latter type. In whatever way it chanced to fall, one spike would point upwards. Surface caltrops were, of course, easier to distribute, but the buried spikes must have been more insidious. Darius planted caltrops on the battlefield at Gaugamela, but Alexander, thanks to information received from a deserter, was able to avoid them.

▲ This illustration copied from a sixth-century Greek vase shows an athlete throwing the javelin. It is interesting to observe the thong wound about the shaft to impart a rotary motion as well as extra leverage. Such thongs were apparently used both in hunting and war, as well as in sport. Alexander made regular use of javelin-throwers in his armies.

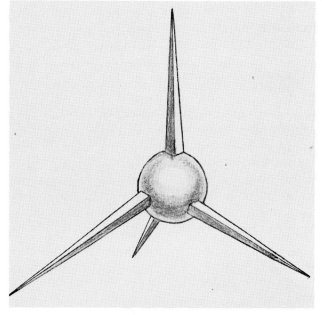

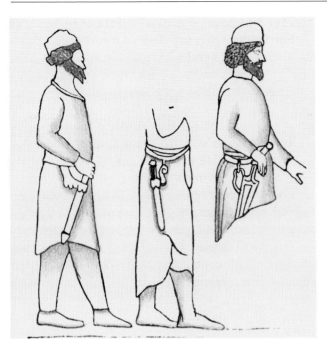

▲ *'Acinaces' is a Persian word, which we know in its Greek form. It has sometimes been translated as 'sabre' or 'scimitar', but more probably it was a short dagger-like sword, such as those shown in this illustration (based on Persepolis reliefs). Swords of this type must also have been used by Alexander's Persian enemies. They certainly appear in sculptures both before and after Alexander's time.*

In none of Alexander's battles were these tactical calculations more evident than at Gaugamela. Knowing that the Macedonian phalanx was virtually certain to be isolated, while he and his cavalry were operating on the far right, he took particular measures to safeguard its position. First he supported it with a rear duplicate formation, which in the event of encirclement could face about and receive an enemy from the reverse direction. He also arranged that the phalanx should be able to extend its line or close ranks at the last minute before battle was joined, and to protect it – at least while this operation was being carried out – he posted curving screens of Agrianes and Macedonian archers on either of its flanks.

In some ancient accounts, it appears that Alexander had overslept on the morning of the battle and that his officers, realizing his need of rest, hesitated to wake him. At any rate, the actual fighting seems to have begun when the sun was well up. The two armies advanced towards each other slowly in line of battle and both sides made cautious and calculated preliminary manoeuvres.

The wide plain completely favoured Darius, giving him every opportunity to exploit his superior numbers. The Persian host far outflanked Alexander's army on either side, but Alexander, determined as always to retain the flanking advantage, led his cavalry off continually towards the right. The Bactrian and Scythian cavalry of Darius's army kept pace with him, extending their line in the same direction. These manoeuvres, however, meant that both sides were drawn away from the central ground that Darius had specially cleared and levelled for use by his chariots, and there was a danger that the chariot fleet would be unable to operate as planned. The King therefore sent orders that his left wing, taking advantage of numbers and greater frontage, should contain Alexander's lateral movement by an enveloping sally, and these orders were duly carried out.

Finding himself thus obstructed, Alexander launched an attack into the middle of the enveloping troops, using for this purpose the mercenary cavalry under Menidas. Scythian and Bactrian troops counter-attacked, but Alexander sent in his Paeonian horse with other mercenaries and temporarily routed them. Even then, reserves of Bactrians arrived and rallied the fugitives. They restored the position, and an equally contested cavalry action resulted, in which Alexander's men suffered serious casualties. They were fighting against great odds, and the Scythians in particular were heavily armoured. However, one wave of Macedonians after another was thrown into the fight and the enemy formations were eventually broken up.

It might be fairly observed that Alexander's flanking moves were often in the nature of a feint and that his attack was timed to catch the enemy in process of reforming to meet the challenge, at a moment when organized response would be most difficult. Tactics of this kind probably opened the battle at Gaugamela, though their success was not immediate.

At this point, Darius threw in his scythe-wheeled chariots. They proved a fiasco, much in the manner of those other scythe-wheeled chariots which had fought three quarters of a century earlier for another Persian king at the battle of Cunaxa. On that occasion, as Xenophon recorded, the Greek troops under attack had simply opened their ranks and allowed the chariots to hurtle through them, plying drivers and horses with missiles as they passed. Alexander's archers and javelin-throwers, who had been stationed forward to screen the cavalry from just such an attack, used similar time-honoured tactics, in some cases seizing the horses' reins and dragging down the drivers. Chariots that passed through unharmed were ultimately isolated and rounded up by the Macedonian hypaspists and grooms.

Such at least is Arrian's account. Other historians present a more gruesome picture of the effect produced by the scythes. But at Gaugamela, the impact of the chariot attack was in any case certainly not decisive; nor does it seem much to have influenced the course of the battle.

Darius, as soon as the chariots had spent their force, or even while they were still in action, made a further attempt to contain Alexander's movement on his left. For Alexander, once his Bactrian and Scythian adversaries had been thrown back, continued to lead his cavalry outward in column.

In a new attempt to block his way, Darius dispatched Persian cavalry from the central sector of his extensive army. This left a gap in the centre,

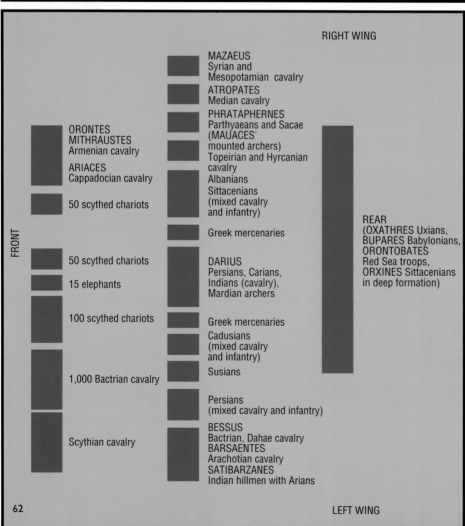

Battle of Gaugamela:
Darius's Order of Battle and Battle Stations

RIGHT WING

MAZAEUS
Syrian and
Mesopotamian cavalry

ATROPATES
Median cavalry

PHRATAPHERNES
Parthyaeans and Sacae
(MAUACES'
mounted archers)

Topeirian and Hyrcanian
cavalry

Albanians

Sittacenians
(mixed cavalry
and infantry)

Greek mercenaries

DARIUS
Persians, Carians,
Indians (cavalry),
Mardian archers

Greek mercenaries

Cadusians
(mixed cavalry
and infantry)

Susians

Persians
(mixed cavalry and infantry)

BESSUS
Bactrian, Dahae cavalry
BARSAENTES
Arachotian cavalry
SATIBARZANES
Indian hillmen with Arians

REAR
(OXATHRES Uxians,
BUPARES Babylonians,
ORONTOBATES
Red Sea troops,
ORXINES Sittacenians
in deep formation)

ORONTES
MITHRAUSTES
Armenian cavalry

ARIACES
Cappadocian cavalry

50 scythed chariots

50 scythed chariots

15 elephants

100 scythed chariots

1,000 Bactrian cavalry

Scythian cavalry

FRONT

LEFT WING

▼ These sculptured spearmen are from the ruins of Persepolis, the Persian capital that Alexander sacked and burnt. The soldiers are seen wearing voluminous gowns over their trousers and jerkins. This explains why the man on the right carries his arrow quiver on his back; the normal Asiatic position for the quiver was on the left hip, but it would have been inconvenient to sling the quiver on the hip either over or under such a gown. 'Kandys' was the Greek name for this flowing robe.

▶ *1. Alexander led the Companion cavalry obliquely in column while the infantry advanced in line of battle. Alexander's move was screened by cavalry and light troops.*

2. Bactrians and Scythians tried to envelop and contain Alexander's move on their flank.

3. Menidas, with mercenary cavalry, on Alexander's orders, tried to break through Persian left.

4. After Menidas was repulsed, Aretas attacked the Bactrians and Scythians.

5. Aretas opened a gap. The Companions attacked in successive waves: they broke through and scattered the enemy.

6. Persians launched chariot attack.

7. Chariot attacks were broken up by archers and Balacrus's light troops.

8. Darius was confronted with the collapse of his left wing and the threat of the advancing pike-phalanx ahead. He fled towards Arbela.

9. Parmenio's cavalry wing, much outnumbered by Mazaeus's horsemen, is on the defensive.

10. Alexander's central infantry moved forward to keep abreast of him and protect his left flank and rear.

11. Consequent gap between infantry and Parmenio's cavalry.

12. Persian and Indian cavalry penetrated the gap, then fanned left and right to attack the Macedonian base camp and surround Parmenio's cavalry.

13. The two left wing pike units were halted by their

Battle of Gaugamela:
Phase 1, Attacks and Counter-attacks (Schematic)

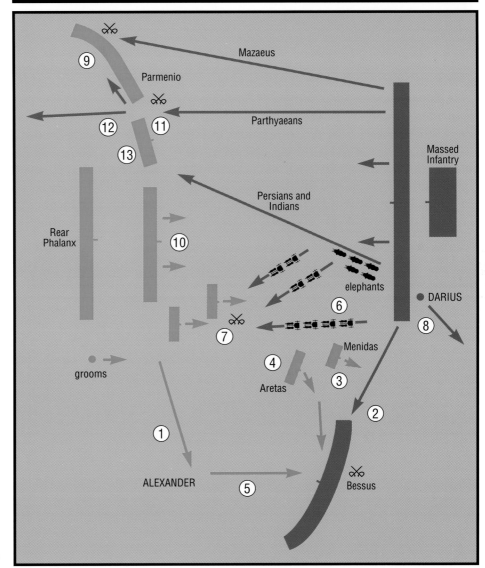

efforts to stem the Persian break-through and to support Parmenio.

Note that the ground in front of Darius's battle line had been levelled to facilitate the movements of his cavalry and chariots, but the extent and location of this pioneer work must remain conjectural.

a fatal weak point, and it no doubt presented the opportunity for which Alexander had been watching – perhaps the false move he had sought to provoke. At once he changed direction and galloped leftwards. Converging with the right-hand units of his own central infantry line, he then led them into the gap with blood-curdling war-cries, making straight for the spot where Darius himself was stationed. Very soon, the Macedonian pikemen were following up.

Darius fled, as he had fled at Issus, so setting the example for his army. It may even be said that he lost the battle by his flight. Meanwhile, Aretes, Alexander's redoubtable cavalry officer, had finally broken up the Persian troops engaged on the Macedonian right wing, and on this sector of the field the Macedonians were entirely victorious. Rout, pursuit and slaughter followed.

On the Macedonian left, however, and in the centre, events had followed a very different course. Only the extreme right-hand unit of pikemen had been able to follow Alexander in his headlong attack upon Darius. The rest had halted in order to sustain their comrades on the left wing, who were in difficulties. A gap inevitably appeared in the pike phalanx, and into this gap Persian cavalry and men of the Indian contingent now poured. They did not attempt to take the phalanx in the

rear, but penetrated deeply, riding straight on, across country, to attack the Macedonian baggage camp. Even allowing for the Persian general advance in the morning, this must have been at any rate four or five miles westward. Invading the camp, they cut down the non-combatant troops who had manned it and liberated Persian prisoners, who now joined in the attack on their former guards.

Apart from those who attacked the camp, some of the Persian cavalry that penetrated the gap in the Macedonian phalanx must have fanned out and threatened Parmenio's left wing from the rear and flank. The danger coincided with an enveloping move launched by the Persian right wing cavalry, and Parmenio's horsemen found themselves menaced by a battle on two fronts. In this desperate situation, Parmenio got a message through to Alexander on the other side of the battlefield urgently appealing for help.

The rear formation of Alexander's phalanx, which had been specially posted and briefed to deal with an enemy break-through of this kind, faced about, raced back to save the camp and at the same time posed a threat to the Persian cavalry that had turned against Parmenio's wing. One would guess that they had to split their forces in order to achieve this double feat.

Again, as at Issus, it was a mark of Alexander's control and discipline that he was able to lead his men back from the easy and rewarding pursuit of a routed enemy into the heat of battle. For this was implied when he responded to Parmenio's appeal. But a confused situation now resulted. In the central plain he collided with the fleeing Persian cavalry, who, as their position deteriorated, were attempting to withdraw. A fierce, congested and chaotic cavalry fight was the result. The effect was certainly to delay Alexander's help for Parmenio. However, the Companion cavalry eventually dispersed the enemy, cutting them down or driving them out of their way. Those who survived fled full-tilt from the battlefield.

▶ *Two types of bow were used in ancient times, the composite and the single-stave bow. The former type was made from two undulant lengths of wood or horn skilfully joined in the middle, and its use probably originated among the Scythians. Alexander more than once found himself involved against Scythian enemies, but also enrolled Scythian archers in his own army.*

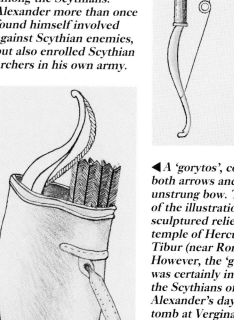

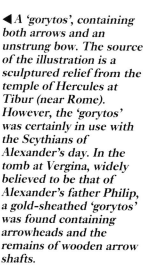

◀ *A 'gorytos', containing both arrows and an unstrung bow. The source of the illustration is a sculptured relief from the temple of Hercules at Tibur (near Rome). However, the 'gorytos' was certainly in use with the Scythians of Alexander's day. In the tomb at Vergina, widely believed to be that of Alexander's father Philip, a gold-sheathed 'gorytos' was found containing arrowheads and the remains of wooden arrow shafts.*

Ultimate Victory

Alexander's relief operation, coupled with that of the rear phalanx, removed the menace to Par-

▶ *In this scene derived from a Greek drinking cup of the fifth century BC, hoplites are arming for battle. Some have already fastened on their corselets, but the third (complete) figure from the left still has shoulder flaps projecting round his ears, waiting to be pulled down and fastened on his chest. The third figure from the right seems to be dismayed by the loss of his helmet crest. If the hoplites Alexander knew, either as friends or enemies, differed from those in the illustration, it was probably in the later style of their helmets rather than in any other article of equipment.*

▶ *This coin is typical of the gold staters issued by Alexander. The helmeted head on the obverse represents the goddess Athena. The helmet is a highly ornate version of the admirably functional Corinthian helmet, which was capable of being pushed to the back of the head for light and air or drawn forward in battle to provide a visor. On the reverse of the coin is the personification of winged Victory holding a wreath.*

prolong the battle after the flight of the king himself.

By the time Alexander approached Parmenio, the most serious threats to the Macedonian left wing had been removed. It was no longer necessary for Alexander to attack Mazaeus, for the Thessalian cavalry, after a heroic resistance under heavy pressure, were now able to take the offensive themselves, and Mazaeus' troops were giving way before them. Alexander turned once more to the pursuit of Darius, and the whole Macedonian army moved forward on the heels of a routed enemy.

The Persian centre had by no means relaxed its flight. Alexander pursued the fugitives until dusk, then crossed the River Lycus and rested his men until midnight. The pursuit was then resumed. Darius, for his part, never stopped to rest.

Parmenio, who in his own sector had lagged only a little behind Alexander in the pursuit, now occupied the Persian camp. The Macedonians' own baggage camp had been saved and the raiders killed or routed, but the seizure of the Persian baggage train with its elephants and camels would have amply compensated them for any losses suffered. Alexander hoped to capture Darius in the town of Arbela 75 miles west of the battlefield; but Darius was not to be found. His abandoned treasure and possessions were seized by Alexander, including – as at Issus – his chariot and weapons.

menio's right, and the Macedonian horse were now better able to cope with the enveloping movement launched by Mazaeus, Darius's cavalry commander on the Persian right wing. Mazaeus had indeed, as he pressed forward, lost touch with the King, and he was for a long while unaware of Darius's flight and of the collapse of the Persian army on the left and in the centre.

The news, when it reached him, inevitably caused him to waver. His attack lost impetus. From his own point of view, there now existed the danger of encirclement. It could be only a matter of time before the Macedonians, already in possession of the central ground, wheeled in his direction. Apart from that, the massive, variously derived Oriental host commanded by the King of Persia was not psychologically conditioned to

Battle of Gaugamela:
Phase 2, Relief Operations (Schematic)

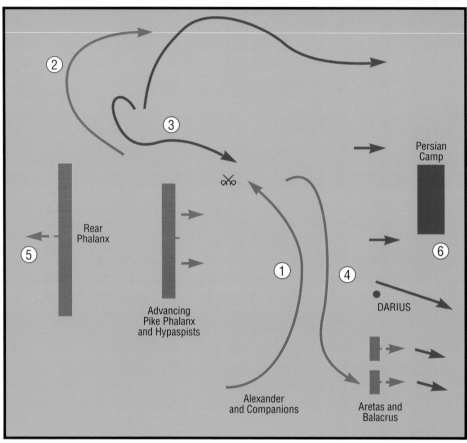

Rear Phalanx

Advancing Pike Phalanx and Hypaspists

Alexander and Companions

Persian Camp

DARIUS

Aretas and Balacrus

Casualty figures for the battle are variously reported by ancient historians, most of them hard to credit. According to Arrian, Alexander lost only 100 dead among his soldiers but over 1,000 horses, half of these animals having been ridden by the Companions. Persian losses are recorded as about 300,000 dead and an even greater number captured. Again, one has to remember that most of the casualties in ancient battles occurred in the course of flight and pursuit.

As at Issus, it may be said that Alexander failed to capture Darius through his own refusal to abandon the centre and left wing of his army in their difficulties. This means that he gave prior consideration where it was due. Ancient history tells of other battles in which the victorious wing of an army has ridden in disorganized and reckless pursuit, only to leave the enemy securely established as victors on the central battlefield.

▲ 1. Parmenio appealed to Alexander for help. Alexander led his victorious Companion cavalry back across the battlefield to relieve him.

2. Mazaeus's attack on Parmenio's wing faltered, probably on news of Darius's flight. Intelligence of Alexander's approach and supporting pressure from left wing Macedonian infantry must also have helped restore the situation. Parmenio took the offensive.

3. Persians and Indians, who had penetrated to Parmenio's rear, attempted to withdraw but collided with Alexander. They were annihilated as a force, but some escaped to follow Darius.

4. Alexander, learning of Parmenio's rally, resumed pursuit of Darius.

5. Other Persians and Indians reached the Macedonian base camp, about five miles distant. They killed many of the guards and released Persian prisoners, but Alexander's rear phalanx turned about and followed them, and after a fight around the camp the raiders were dispersed.

6. Parmenio, following Mazaeus's fugitive troops, captured the Persian camp. Alexander pursued Darius as far as Arbela, but Darius once more eluded him.

Note that when Alexander turned with his Companion cavalry to relieve Parmenio, he presumably left troops in the rear of the fugitive Persian left wing to ensure that it did not rally and re-form. The units commanded by Aretas and Balacrus were perhaps charged with this responsibility. The mercenary cavalry under Menidas was with Alexander in the central clash, in which Menidas was himself wounded.

▲These warriors are characteristic of the Scythians at the time of Alexander's campaigns. The Scythians had their own independent kingdom north of the Black Sea and proved dangerous opponents for both the Persians and the Macedonians. They also provided some of the best mercenary light cavalry in the ancient world, fighting at various times for both Darius and Alexander. (Painting by Angus McBride)

THE BACTRIAN YEARS

It was to be almost five years before Alexander would fight another glorious pitched battle; instead, during much of that time he would be occupied with strenuous guerilla fighting and mountain warfare. Darius fled north-eastward into the mountains of Media, guessing rightly that Alexander would immediately turn his attention to the great central cities of the empire, which lay to the south: Babylon, Susa and Persepolis.

Alexander was well received at Babylon and Susa, and his treatment of the population was accordingly generous, but he had to fight for Persepolis, first against Uxian mountain tribes, then against Persian regular forces. When he captured the city, he burnt it. This act of destruction may not have been premeditated: according to some accounts, it was a result of wild caprice, the product of a drinking bout in the company of a courtesan.

Before moving north again through Media in pursuit of Darius, Alexander placed governors over the territory he had recently conquered. These included Persian administrators, and one may discern here a new policy, a foretaste perhaps of those war aims of universal citizenship he was later to embrace when the mere destruction of an enemy seemed no longer to justify the time, trouble and suffering involved. But Darius at this time still seemed bent on some kind of resistance. He had collected around him the semblance of an army, with about 2,000 Greek mercenaries, and could if necessary fall back east of the Caspian then northwards into the Bactrian mountains.

In the event, Alexander never took Darius alive. He was not in time to prevent the Persian king escaping through the Caspian pass into the northern mountains. As the pursuing Macedonian army rested briefly in camp, news came that Darius had been forcibly seized by a group of his own officers, among whom was Bessus, satrap of Bactria, a relative of the King. Bessus had obvious claims – which he soon asserted – to rule over the rump of the Persian Empire. He had commanded the Bactrian contingent at Gaugamela, and there was a likelihood that Alexander might find him a more formidable enemy than Darius.

It was important to forestall a resurgence of Persian opposition. Alexander at once left his main army and pressed on in the tracks of the fugitives with a small, highly mobile body of troops. The men of his advance party eventually discovered Darius on the point of death, mortally wounded by his captors when they found that they could no longer drag him with them in their flight. Alexander arranged a royal funeral for Darius; later, when he captured Bessus, he was to hand the pretender over to Darius's brother Oxathres for barbarous execution.

The problem of war aims now became acute. The populations of Bactria and Sogdiana, northwards, which were loosely attached provinces of the Persian Empire, still seemed determined to fight for their independence. But before making any northerly advance, Alexander pursued the Greek mercenaries who had served under Darius and forced their surrender when he overtook them in Hyrcania, south of the Caspian Sea.

However, Alexander's ideal of a mixed Asiatic and European nationality did not appeal to his men, and he soon faced conspiracies among his officers and immediate entourage. He executed Philotas, the son of his once-trusted second-in-command Parmenio, then as precaution arranged the murder of Parmenio, whom he had left in charge of the Median garrison. In a drunken brawl, he later killed Clitus, the officer who had saved his life at the Granicus. In fact, Alexander often appeared now in the role of a tyrant – a role in which many ancient historians of later centuries consistently saw him. Nevertheless, the rank and file of his army still followed him devotedly.

After the capture of Bessus (329BC), which had occurred in Sogdiana, north of the River Oxus, a new leader of resistance emerged in the person of Spitamenes, a Bactrian nobleman. It might truthfully be said that Spitamenes was the most redoubtable enemy that Alexander ever had to face. The Bactrian leader's flexible guerrilla tactics implemented with the support of Scythian allies from across the River Jaxartes, cost the Macedonians many lives. In fact, in one devastating ambush alone, more of Alexander's men fell than in all his glorious pitched battles put together.

Little by little, however, Alexander garrisoned the north-eastern provinces against his wily enemies. Spitamenes summoned to his aid the Massagetae, a warlike Scythian tribe who lived east of the Caspian Sea. But when defeated by Alexander, the Scythians murdered Spitamenes and sent his head to the victor as a peace offering. (Another account has it that Spitamenes was murdered by his wife.) At Maricanda (Samarkand), Alexander married Roxana, the daughter of a Sogdian nobleman. She had been taken prisoner by the Macedonians and was a famed beauty. Apart from its immediate political convenience, this marriage was in line with Alexander's emerging war aims – the forging of a Eurasian nation and a Greco-Asiatic culture. The fact that Alexander had previously married Stateira, Darius's daughter, at Susa was no impediment to the Sogdian wedding: Macedonian kings did not profess monogamy, and in this respect at least they were 'unGreek'.

The years of Alexander's fighting in the north-eastern provinces of the Persian Empire are recorded by historians in some detail, though with many discrepancies. We hear of battles and of treachery, rapid marches and river crossings, the scaling of cliffs and the capture of daunting mountain strongholds, with feats of arms in the course of which Alexander was more than once wounded. At this time more than any, the sum of effort and hardship suffered by the conquering army seems great and out of all proportion to any useful purpose served.

However, by dint of war and diplomacy, Alexander at last subdued the intransigent population. He secured the whole territory by planting garrisons of Macedonian and Greek soldiers. The Scythians north of the Jaxartes were a permanent menace. They had once been denizens of the lands the Persians later controlled, and there was also a danger that they might make common cause with any resurgent movement in the north-east provinces themselves. Before marching southwards, across the 'Indian Caucasus' (Hindu Kush), Alexander left outposts of rather war-weary men to hold the frontier of the Jaxartes and the town he had founded there – 'Alexandria-Eschatē' – that is to say, 'Farthest Alexandria'.

He was now destined for the River Indus. In planning his expedition into India, Alexander pitched his ambitions even beyond the confines of the old Persian Empire. At this point, if any, Alexander's men could be expected to show those symptoms of mutiny that were later to frustrate him. But the army, reassured by legends of the god Dionysus's visit to India, followed their leader into the Indus valley without demur.

Alexander did not in fact immediately attempt a crossing of the great river, but during the winter of 327/326 he spent his time campaigning against hill tribes in the mountainous region towards modern Chitral. His officer Hephaestion was sent by a route farther south and had contrived to bridge the Indus before Alexander rejoined him. Arrian, on the analogy of Roman bridging operations in his own time, suggests convincingly that Hephaestion's bridge was laid on pontoons.

Beyond the Indus, the Macedonians were well received by the ruler of Taxila, who is named in Arrian's history as Taxiles. His real name was probably 'Amphi', and the title 'Taxiles' derived from the name of his chief city. He submitted to Alexander of his own accord, no doubt seeing in the invaders allies against the king farther east, whom the Greeks knew as Porus (Pŏros). While resting his troops at Taxila, Alexander received the submission of other Indian rulers, but it soon became evident that in making a friend of Taxiles he had assured himself of the enmity of Porus; accordingly, intent upon a new war, he now marched east again towards the River Hydaspes (modern Jhelum), beyond which Porus was mobilizing his army.

THE BATTLE OF THE HYDASPES

When Alexander reached the Hydaspes, he found King Porus's substantial army ranged against him on the opposite bank. In ancient times, it often happened that battles were fought at river crossings: not only was a river a defensive moat, it was also a water supply for the troops encamped on its banks. The Hydaspes in any case was not a mere torrent or mountain stream, nor even a river of moderate size such as could be forded easily at suitable points. At this time of year in particular it

Battle of the Hydaspes: Strategy

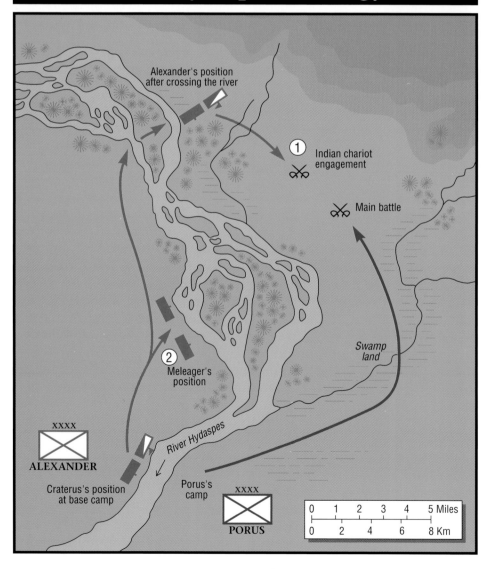

1. The preliminary Indian chariot attack: Porus' son (his brother, according to Curtius, with 4,000 cavalry), with a body of 2,000 cavalry and 120 chariots, was sent to oppose Alexander's crossing. This force would have been enough if it had been in time (i.e., while the Macedonians were still floundering in the river). But Alexander had already landed 5,000 cavalry and 6,000 infantry. The prince, finding himself outnumbered, tried to withdraw, but the Indian force was overtaken and dispersed with the loss of 400 cavalry. All chariots were captured and the prince killed.

2. Craterus and Meleager held the line of the river and immobilized the Indian troops that might otherwise have been led off to confront Alexander. When Alexander was victorious, Craterus and Meleager, acting on orders, led their men across the river and intercepted the fugitives.

▶ *It is inferred (though not explicitly stated by Arrian) that Meleager, Attalus and Gorgias were in command of their own pike units as well as the mercenary troops they led on this occasion. The hipparchy that was under nominal or administrative command of Perdiccas seems to have been that which Coenus led in the actual battle. Perdiccas himself was accompanying Alexander as a bodyguard. The Parapamisidae had been recruited from the 'Indian Caucasus' (i.e., Hindu Kush). A hipparchy was about 1,000 strong. The Hypaspists consisted of 3 units, each about 1,000 strong. A pike unit ('taxis') was about 1,500 strong. Alexander had about 1,000 horse-bowmen with him in the battle.*

■ *Note that 'Hydaspes' is a Greek attempt at the ancient Indian name 'Vidasta'. The Muslim invaders of later centuries called the river the Jihlam (Jhelum) after the town that stood on its banks. The town of Jihlam is probably close to the site of Alexander's base camp.*

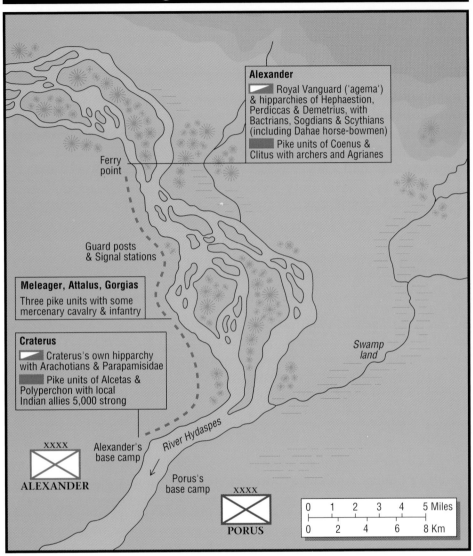

Battle of the Hydaspes:
The River Crossing and Alexander's Order of Battle

Alexander

▭ Royal Vanguard ('agema') & hipparchies of Hephaestion, Perdiccas & Demetrius, with Bactrians, Sogdians & Scythians (including Dahae horse-bowmen)

▬ Pike units of Coenus & Clitus with archers and Agrianes

Ferry point

Guard posts & Signal stations

Meleager, Attalus, Gorgias

Three pike units with some mercenary cavalry & infantry

Craterus

▭ Craterus's own hipparchy with Arachotians & Parapamisidae

▬ Pike units of Alcetas & Polyperchon with local Indian allies 5,000 strong

Swamp land

River Hydaspes

XXXX
ALEXANDER
Alexander's base camp

Porus's base camp

XXXX
PORUS

0	1	2	3	4	5 Miles
0	2	4	6	8 Km	

was a full-flowing navigable waterway.

Nevertheless, the opposing armies were perfectly visible to each other across the broad waters, which as the result of seasonal conditions were now, in early summer, swift and turbulent. The numerical strength of Porus's army is variously recorded by different ancient historians, and modern accounts do not always agree in the interpretation of the figures. The main body of the Indian army seems to have numbered between 20,000 and 50,000 infantry, between 2,000 and 4,000 cavalry, anything from 85 to 200 elephants

and from 300 to more than 1,000 chariots. It is additionally reported that Porus's brother was present with a force of 4,000 cavalry and 100 chariots. Margins of difference are therefore considerable, and one must be forgiven for assuming midway figures.

Alexander, apart from a force of 5,000 Indian allies, now led other Asiatic troops from farther west, but the core of his army was still that body of Macedonian infantry and Companion cavalry with which he had crossed the Hellespont, and the army with which he faced Porus was probably no more than 40,000 strong. He had always found that such a number gave him strategic and tactical mobility, and he had proved that it was capable of defeating in battle Asiatic forces of any size that could be brought against it.

With the Hydaspes in flood, there was, of course, no immediate possibility of fording the river. Alexander gave out publicly that he was content to wait for the autumn months when the water would run very much lower. No doubt he intended that such pronouncements should come to the ears of the enemy – but it is quite evident that he had laid other plans.

Porus strongly guarded all possible ferry crossings, and his elephants became extremely useful in this role, for they would certainly terrify any horses that confronted them, making a cavalry landing from rafts or barges quite out of the question. But Alexander was, as ever, resourceful. Before moving up to the frontiers of Porus's territory, he had dismantled the boats and galleys he had used on the Indus. The smaller craft had been broken into two, the thirty-oar galleys into three, parts; the sections had then been transported on wagons overland and the whole flotilla reassembled on the Hydaspes. From the first, these boats had been able to navigate the river unmolested, the Indians having made no attempt to deny them the use of the midway channel.

During the weeks that followed, Alexander moved his cavalry continually up and down the river bank with as much commotion as possible. Porus, to forestall the concentration of Alexander's troops at any single point, dispatched forces to march level with Alexander's men on the opposite bank, guided by the noise the Macedonians deliberately created. Any place at which a crossing seemed contemplated was immediately guarded in strength by the Indians. Alexander's movements, however, were mere feints. No attack materialized, and in the end Porus relaxed his vigilance. This, of course, was Alexander's intention. The Macedonians were now in a position to make a real attack. Any sound of their movements would inevitably be discounted by the enemy as another false alert.

Alexander's cavalry as it moved up and down the river bank in the course of its diversionary tactics, had at the same time reconnoitred for suitable crossing places and had reported to Alexander. He now selected what seemed a suitable point and planned to cross the river by night. He left his officer Craterus in the area where the Macedonian army had originally encamped, with the cavalry unit (hipparchy) this officer normally commanded, as well as attached units of Asiatic cavalry and local Indian troops to the number of 5,000, plus two units of the Macedonian phalanx.

Alexander himself set out for the chosen crossing place with a similarly mixed but stronger force. It included the vanguard of the Companion cavalry and the cavalry units of his officers, Hephaestion, Perdiccas and Demetrius. These units were 'hipparchies', of greater strength than the squadrons he had used in Asia Minor. He also led Asiatic troops that included mounted archers, and two phalanx units with archers and Agrianes.

The purpose of leaving a substantial force at the base camp was, of course, to disguise from Porus the fact that he had moved. The Indians must know nothing of his crossing until it was an accomplished fact. His orders to Craterus were that if Porus led away only part of his army to meet the emergency, leaving a force of elephants behind him, then the Macedonians at the base camp should remain where they were, still covering the enemy on the opposite bank. If, on the other hand, Porus abandoned his present position entirely, either in flight or to face Alexander, then Craterus and his men might safely cross. In fact, the main danger to the Macedonian cavalry was from the elephants. Once these were withdrawn, the river might confidently be crossed, no matter what other Indian troops remained.

Night Operations

The point selected as a crossing place was about eighteen miles upstream from the base camp. Here, on the opposite bank, was a headland where the river bent, covered with luxuriant undergrowth, and in the river alongside it rose an island, also densely forested, such as would conceal the proximity or even the presence of cavalry. Along the bank, on the Macedonian side, Alexander had already posted a chain of pickets, capable of communicating with each other either by means of visual or audible signals. In conformity with his previous practice, he had allowed the enemy to become accustomed to the shouts and nightly watchfires of these outposts.

Screened by such diversions, Alexander's march was made in great secrecy. It followed an inland route, though this does not mean that it was circuitous. On the contrary, an inland track between two sharp river bends may very easily be a short cut. As the Macedonians marched through the night, they were overtaken by a thunderstorm with heavy rain. Though they cannot have enjoyed it, the storm must have helped render their movements imperceptible to the enemy.

At the crossing place a ferry fleet had been prepared in advance. Many of the ferries were rafts floated on skins that had been transported empty to the spot, then stuffed with chaff and sewn up in such a way as to be watertight. Alexander had previously used this technique for ferrying troops both on the Danube and on the Oxus. But now he also had thirty-oar galleys, which had been in service on the Indus. These had again been transported in sections overland and reassembled at the place where they were required.

Close to the river bank, at an intermediate position between the base camp and the ferry point, he stationed his three officers, Meleager, Attalus and Gorgias, each in charge of his own infantry unit, with attached cavalry and infantry detailed from among the mercenaries. Like Craterus, this force was ordered to cross only when it saw that the enemy on the opposite bank of the river was committed elsewhere. The crossing was to be made in three waves. It is easy to guess that the ferry craft at their disposal were not enough to permit a transit in one body.

At dawn the storm subsided. The ferry flotilla, as it moved out into the river, led by Alexander and his staff in a thirty-oar galley, was at first out of sight from the other bank. But as they went farther they were obliged to break cover, and enemy scouts galloped off to report their approach. Alexander's men now ran into unforeseen difficulties. For the bank that had seemed to be the mainland opposite in reality belonged to another island. A deep but narrow channel separated it from the land beyond, and men and animals barely managed to ford the fast-flowing current – sometimes with little more than their heads above water.

Emerging at last from this second crossing, Alexander was able to marshal his troops unmolested by the enemy and without difficulty on the mainland. As far as it is possible to interpret a debatable ancient text, it seems that he now advanced with the river on his right (i.e., downstream) to face Porus's army, and that he marched in semi-deployed formation. The Companions, with all the best cavalry, were massed in front of the infantry, and ahead of these were 1,000 horse-bowmen, serving as a screen and equipped, be it noticed, to deal with elephants at long range. The main cavalry, about 5,000 in number, were provided with a flank guard of archers under the command of Tauron, who was ordered for the time being to keep up with the horses as best he could.

Behind the cavalry marched the hypaspists under Seleucus. The main pike phalanx, marching in battle line, was guarded by Agrianes and javelin-throwers on both its flanks. We are not told the position of cavalry units that had not been selected for a forward role: either they must have followed, at this stage, in the rear or guarded the left flank of the hypaspists.

Arrian suggests that Alexander was willing, if occasion arose, to challenge Porus's whole army with his cavalry alone, but this can hardly have been so. Apart from anything else, the whole object of Alexander's tactics was to avoid confronting his cavalry with elephants. He must have led his mounted troops forward simply to repel any cavalry or chariot attack upon the disembarkation point. Indeed, the ferry operation was not complete, even after the landing of his main body. He had not been able to transport all his forces in a single crossing of the river. The infantry with which he first disembarked numbered about 6,000, certainly less a number than that with which he had set out from the base camp.

The Indian Reaction

When news of the crossing reached Porus, the Indian king did not believe that it had been made

1 *After weeks of diversionary manoeuvring in the face of Porus's elephants on the opposite bank, Alexander led his striking force of cavalry and infantry upstream to make the crossing. Night, storm and jungle concealed his initiative from the enemy.*

2 *Craterus was left with a holding force, still facing Porus's elephants.*

3 *Meleager, with Gorgias and Attalus, was left in a midway position. They were to cross the river with their troops in three waves – only when victory was seen to be assured on the opposite bank.*

4 *At the planned crossing point, a fleet of ships and barges (already transported overland in prefabricated sections) awaited Alexander. But he landed on an island he had mistaken for a* promontory of the farther bank, and his men were obliged to wade across a second channel, sometimes neck-deep.

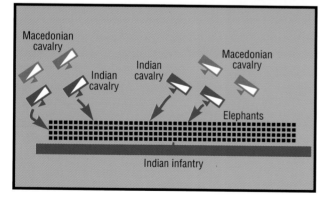

SITE OF
MODERN
MUNGLA

ALEXANDER

Battle of the Hydaspes: The Elephant Line

Macedonian cavalry

Indian cavalry

Indian cavalry

Macedonian cavalry

Elephants

Indian infantry

▲ *The diagram shows 200 elephants stationed at 100-foot intervals. The arrangement in four ranks, giving a front one mile long, is conjectural. The purpose is merely to illustrate the role of the* elephant line as a mobile fortress. It served the Indian cavalry and infantry either as a refuge into which they could retreat or as a base from which they could sally. Under pressure of missile attack, the elephant line was broken and contracted. Those who had sheltered within its ranks became casualties among the stampeding elephants.

Both Diodorus and Curtius compare the elephant line to a walled city with its towers raised at intervals. Arrian says that the Indian infantry companies projected for a short distance into the intervals among the elephants. Diodorus compares the infantry to curtain walls between towering elephants. The diagram also shows the Indian horsemen racing for shelter in the elephant line to escape the onslaught of Alexander and Coenus.

5 *Alexander marshalled his forces. He led his main cavalry on the right; his left was lightly held.*
6 *Soon after landing, he was attacked by a force of Indian cavalry and chariots, but routed them with heavy loss.*

THE CROSSING OF THE HYDASPES
Manoeuvres on the river banks leading to battle, May 326BC

7 *Continuing on his downstream march to meet Porus, he found time to rest his men.*

8 *Porus, learning that Alexander had crossed the river in force, marched to meet him, leaving part of his forces,* including some elephants, to face Craterus. Alexander opened battle with an attack by mounted archers.

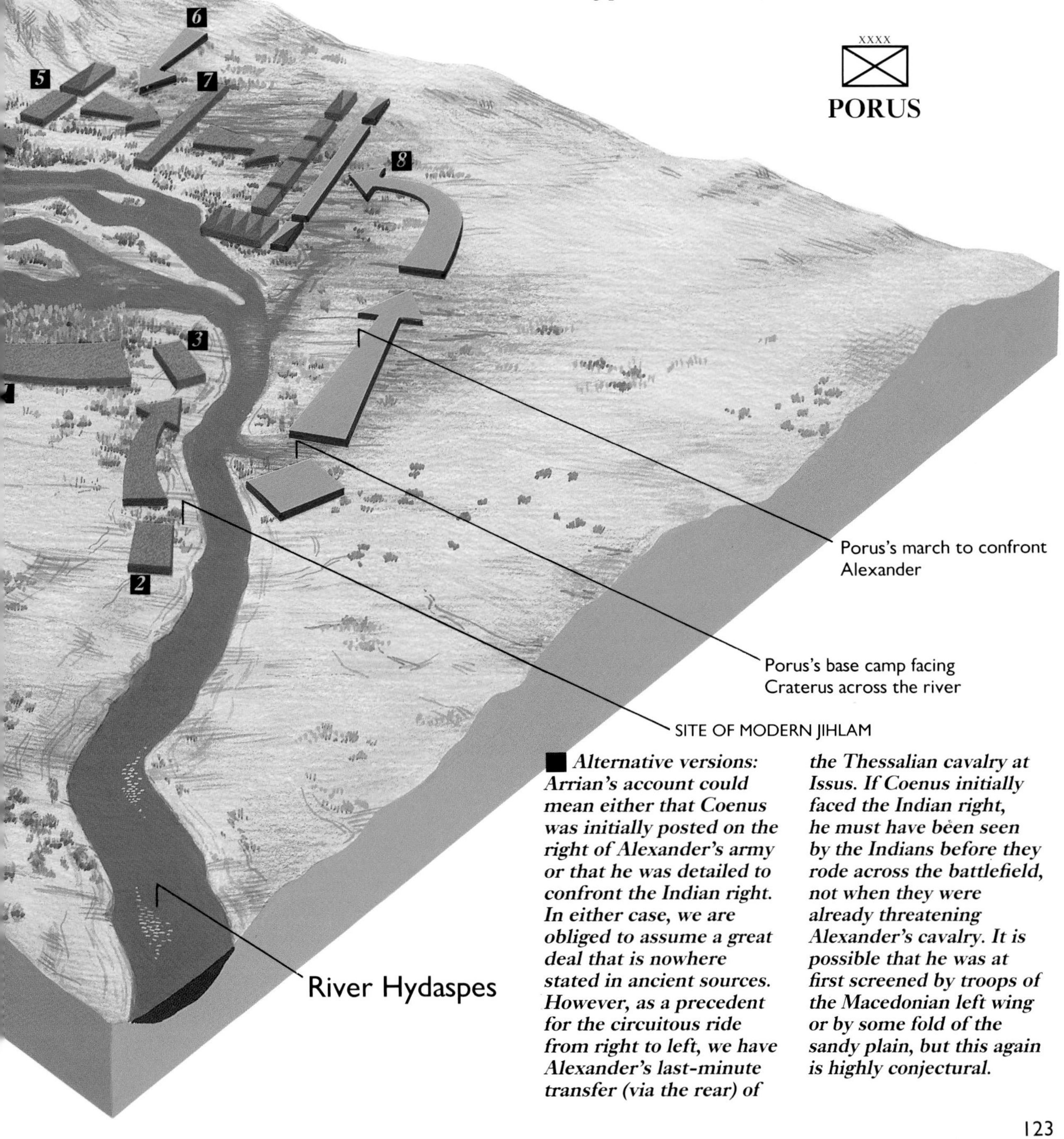

xxxx

PORUS

Porus's march to confront Alexander

Porus's base camp facing Craterus across the river

SITE OF MODERN JIHLAM

River Hydaspes

■ *Alternative versions: Arrian's account could mean either that Coenus was initially posted on the right of Alexander's army or that he was detailed to confront the Indian right. In either case, we are obliged to assume a great deal that is nowhere stated in ancient sources. However, as a precedent for the circuitous ride from right to left, we have Alexander's last-minute transfer (via the rear) of* the Thessalian cavalry at Issus. If Coenus initially faced the Indian right, he must have been seen by the Indians before they rode across the battlefield, not when they were already threatening Alexander's cavalry. It is possible that he was at first screened by troops of the Macedonian left wing or by some fold of the sandy plain, but this again is highly conjectural.

in strength, and he thought that a mobile force dispatched under the leadership of his son, would be enough to cope with the situation. He could, after all, see Craterus's men still encamped opposite him on the other side of the river, and he imagined that these represented the Macedonian main army. Alexander had in fact planned and hoped that he should believe precisely this. The Indian detachment sent against Alexander numbered only some 2,000 cavalry and 120 chariots. These at least are the figures recorded by Alexander's officer Ptolemy and accepted by Arrian. The chariot force was in any case immediately routed, with a reported loss of 400 killed – among whom was the young prince. Horses and chariots were mainly captured.

Porus now realized that he would have to march against Alexander with the greater part of his army. However, Craterus's troops, already preparing to cross the river in force, could not be disregarded, and the Indian king left a small body of men to guard the river bank, with some elephants, which he hoped would be enough to daunt any oncoming Macedonian cavalry. He himself moved with his main army against Alexander. His army numbered about 4,000 cavalry, 300 chariots, 200 elephants and 30,000 infantry. Much of the country over which he marched was muddy and difficult, but finding a sandy plain that would give his cavalry freedom of manoeuvre he halted and made ready for battle.

The Indian front line was composed of elephants, stationed at approximately 100-foot intervals. Behind the elephants and in the intervals between them were more infantry, guarded on their exposed flanks by cavalry and further screened by war chariots at each end of the whole front. When Alexander came within sight of the Indian battle array, he halted and allowed his infantry to rest, while the cavalry patrolled around them.

Before going into action against Porus, Alexander reshuffled the leadership of his own army. His senior officers were variously assignable – their individual competence not limited to any one arm of the fighting forces. Coenus was appointed to command of Demetrius's cavalry, Demetrius being perhaps retained as second-in-command.

Seleucus remained in charge of the hypaspists. But the leaders of the pike phalanx were now Tauron and Antigenes. Since such changes were possible, it is easy to see how they might become desirable at this stage. Fighting a battle is a different sort of operation from crossing a river and might reasonably call for changes of leadership.*

Porus enjoyed an overwhelming superiority in infantry numbers, but Alexander had the advantage in cavalry. In any case, the whole issue depended on whether the Macedonian cavalry could be engaged by the Indian elephants and thrown into confusion or whether such a confrontation could be avoided. Alexander avoided it. He opened the battle with an attack by his horse-bowmen, which produced considerable disorder in the enemy's left wing formations.

It should be remembered that Porus's chariots had been marshalled on each wing ahead of his cavalry. The chariots on his left must have borne the first impact of Alexander's mounted bowmen. They presumably presented large targets to the attackers, for each chariot is reported as carrying six men – only two of whom bore shields.

It seems that the Indian king now had second thoughts about the deployment of his army, for an attempt was made to lead his cavalry out in front of the chariots. But Alexander with his Companion cavalry fell upon the Indian left wing horsemen while they were still advancing in column and before they had time to deploy into line of battle. The whole of Porus's left wing was now forced on to the defensive.

On the other side of the field, the right wing cavalry of the Indians did their best to save the situation. They swept across the central plain to counter-attack against Alexander's flank. Any opposing horsemen on the left flank of the Macedonian infantry must have been too few or too far off to discourage the Indian manoeuvre. But Alexander's officer Coenus, acting on a pre-arranged plan, now detached himself from the other Companions and led his cavalry in a circuitous ride – presumably at a gallop – to emerge on the tail of the counter-attacking Indians

---

* For other interpretations of the ancient sources on this subject, see P. A. Brunt, 'Alexander's Macedonian Cavalry' in *The Journal of Hellenic Studies*, vol. LXXXIII, 1963.

in their transverse career across the battlefield. It cannot be excluded that in order to carry out this operation Coenus actually passed to the rear of the advancing Macedonian infantry before the enemy observed his approach. He certainly came into view suddenly and unexpectedly, when the Indian right wing cavalry was already almost at grips with Alexander's Companions.

The Indians were, of course, now threatened with battle on two fronts – it could not be avoided. They reacted by dividing their forces and facing in two directions simultaneously, against Alexander and against Coenus. This meant reforming. But Alexander suddenly wheeled inwards and charged them as they were in the middle of their man- oeuvre. Without attempting to withstand the full onslaught of the Companion cavalry, they fell back for cover among the elephants.

The Defeat of Porus

The elephants certainly now proved their value. Nor was their role purely defensive, and they went forward against the oncoming Macedonian in- fantry despite showers of missiles from Alex- ander's archers and javelin-throwers. They savagely mangled the pike phalanx, trampling enemies underfoot or using their tusks and trunks in a way that must have owed some of its effectiveness to military training.

The Indian horsemen now briefly took heart again and made a final sally against Alexander's cavalry, but they were driven back once more among the elephants. The battle at this stage wore an unusual aspect, for the cavalry of both sides, instead of being distributed on either wing, was concentrated as a dense and confused mass in the centre.

The attack of the elephants soon lost its momentum, however. Their drivers were vulner- able to javelins and arrows, and the Macedonians were in a position to give way before them as prudence dictated then renew their offensive when the animals tired. The elephants were also often wounded and maddened to a point at which they were out of control, even where they had not lost their drivers.

The Indian cavalry was, in contrast to the Macedonians, penned in an ever-contracting area among the elephants. It was a common experience of ancient warfare that frightened elephants, out of control, would do as much damage to their own masters as to the enemy. Porus's elephants on this occasion were no exception: the Indians, jostling and huddling among them, were trampled and crushed. Meanwhile, the Indian infantry, deprived of any support from cavalry, elephants or chariots, were no match for the Macedonian pike phalanx as it came on against them with shields locked together.

At last, when all arms of Porus's forces were exhausted, Alexander's cavalry and infantry moved in, surrounding and capturing the elephants, which had now been reduced to a stationary role, trumpeting and bellowing in pathetic protest. In this action, the Indian cavalry was annihilated as a fighting force, and those of Porus's men who discovered a merciful gap in the encircling enemy lines took to flight. Flight, however, did not easily save them. For Craterus and the other Mace- donians posted on the west bank of the Hydaspes now crossed the river and intercepted the ex- hausted fugitives.

Porus, a gigantic man, mounted on an elephant and protected by a stout corselet, had, unlike Darius, continued fighting until the end. Only when he was wounded and faint did he abandon the struggle. Alexander sent his own ally, the Indian King Taxiles, to pursue Porus and invite his surrender, but Porus, from the back of his elephant, threatened Taxiles with a spear and drove him away. A second ambassador was sent, whose relations with Porus had in the past been happier. The Indian king was at last induced to dismount from his elephant and parley with Alexander, who, full of admiration for a gallant enemy, and probably also alive to diplomatic considerations, granted him the honourable terms he demanded and concluded an alliance with him.

In the battle and the pursuit that ensued 3,000 Indian cavalry were reported lost, 20,000 infantry were killed, and all the chariots were wrecked. Surviving elephants became the booty of the victors. Again, we are left with the impression that an ancient battle was a kind of violent athletic event, in which massacre was the penalty of defeat.

▶ 1. Alexander's horse-bowmen rained arrows on Indian left wing cavalry.

2. Indian cavalry, unwilling to remain sitting targets for horse-bowmen, sallied against them.

3. Alexander's Companions charged the Indian cavalry as they rode out in column (i.e., before they could deploy) and threw them into confusion.

4. Indian right wing cavalry rode transversely to support the threatened Indian left.

5. Coenus emerged unexpectedly to attack the Indian right wing cavalry in the rear, as it moved across the field.

6. Part of the Indian right wing cavalry were diverted to meet Coenus' attack.

After this the Indian cavalry, fighting on two fronts, was forced back among the elephants – which themselves had come under attack from Alexander's advancing Agrianes and archers, with resulting confusion and defeat of the Indians. All chariots were destroyed and elephants captured or killed.

◀ An Indian war elephant similar to those used by Porus at the River Hydaspes. (Painting by Richard Geiger)

Indian numbers and casualty figures according to the main ancient sources

Numbers engaged in the main battle

	Cavalry	Chariots	Elephants	Infantry
Arrian	4,000	300	200	30,000
Quintus Curtius Rufus	not given	300	85	30,000
Diodorus Siculus	3,000	over 1,000	130	50,000
Plutarch	2,000	not given	not given	20,000

Numbers engaged in opening encounter with Porus' son (brother?)

Aristobulus (as cited by Arrian)		60
Ptolemy (as cited by Arrian)	2,000	120
Plutarch	1,000	60
Quintus Curtius Rufus	4,000	100

Casualties

	Cavalry	Chariots	Elephants	Infantry
Arrian	3,000	all chariots	all killed or captured	20,000
Diodorus Siculus	not known	not known	85 captured	not known

Diodorus also says that total Indian casualties were 12,000 killed and 9,000 captured and that Macedonian casualties were 280 cavalry and 700 infantry killed. Arrian's report of Macedonian casualty figures gives an aggregate of 230 cavalry and 80 infantry killed.

Battle of the Hydaspes: Tactics

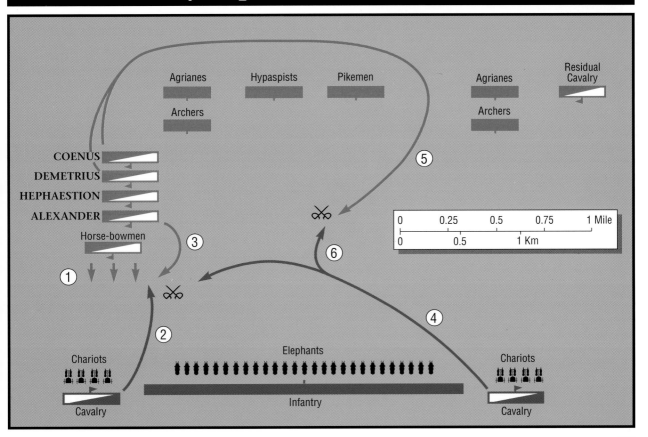

BACK TO BABYLON

Alexander made an ally of Porus and reconciled him with Taxiles. Beside the Hydaspes, he founded two new towns, Nicaea and Bucephala, the latter named after his famous warhorse, which here died of old age. He rested his men for a month, and about this time received reinforcements of Thracian troops drafted by his governor in the Caspian area. Hearing of disaffection in Assacenia, a mountainous territory (identified with modern Bajaur and Swat), which he had previously conquered on his march to the Indus valley, he dispatched troops to restore the situation.

But Alexander was now defied by a second Indian king called Porus. (One may suspect that the Greek form of the name represents what was an Indian title.) The second Porus soon fled from Alexander's advance, but Alexander eagerly pursued him, crossing the turbulent River Acesines (Chenab) and the calmer Hydraotes (Ravi). This brought him into conflict with the tribe of the Cathaei, and the subsequent hostilities again called for the exercise of his versatile military genius. He then marched to the River Hyphasis (Beas).

It is suggested in Arrian's pages that Alexander had hopes of reaching the 'Ocean Stream', which according to Greek geographic preconceptions, encircled the land mass of the world. However, his men now followed him with ever-waning enthusiasm. When he observed their flagging morale, he attempted to rally them with an impassioned appeal; after the prolonged silence that greeted Alexander's oratory, Coenus courageously voiced the reluctance of the army. This made Alexander angry with the army in general and Coenus in particular, and he thereupon sulked in his tent for two days. When the soldiers showed no remorse at having wounded his susceptibilities, he realized that the time for a more or less gracious withdrawal had at last come.

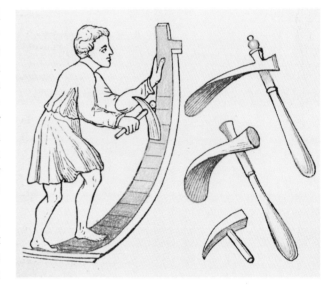

▲ *Alexander both employed in his army and recruited locally skilled artificers. The adze (in Greek 'skeparnon') was a tool constantly in use. Its application in shipbuilding is attested by this figure, and it will be remembered how effectively river fleets were constructed, dismantled and transported in sections during the Indian campaign.*

▼ *These illustrations show a type of broad-brimmed Macedonian hat known as a 'Causia'. The figure on the left is taken from a Greek vase, and that on the right is from a medal of Alexander I of Macedon. A similar broad-brimmed hat, worn by a mounted figure, appears on coins of Philip II of Macedon, and Alexander III (the Great) is known to have worn such a hat.*

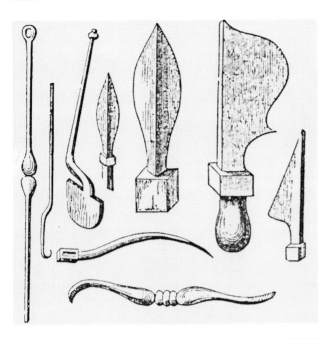

◀ *These illustrations of surgical instruments are based on collections of instruments found at Pompeii, but those used by the medical staff in Alexander's army cannot have been very different. In India, Alexander himself would probably have died if it had not been possible to extract an enemy arrowhead that had entered his body. The operation was said by some writers to have been carried out by Critodemus of Cos, a professional medical man, though by other accounts one of Alexander's bodyguards cut out the arrowhead with his sword, no medical help being available at the time.*

brought scaling ladders against the enemy walls, Alexander himself seized a ladder and appeared on the battlements single-handed, a magnificent sky-line target. Realizing his exposed position, he leapt down within the walls of the citadel and virtually challenged the whole garrison – still single-handed. He was struck down and all but mortally wounded. One of his officers* in rescuing him was killed. In the nick of time the Macedonians broke down the gate below. Alexander very nearly died on this occasion, and the Macedonians in vengeance massacred every man, woman and child in the captured town.

While recovering from his almost fatal wound, Alexander directed the construction of a large fleet on the Hydaspes, and in command of this fleet he found his way downstream to the Acesines and so at last to the Indus. Military and political considerations had led him to dispatch Craterus and his main army on a homeward march through Arachosia and the city of Alexandria (Kandahar) that had been founded there. Alexander himself, however, was now bent upon exploration and discovery. He assembled his remaining troops and accompanying fleet at Pattala at the head of the Indus delta, preparatory to a double homeward expedition made concurrently by land and sea.

Before setting out, Alexander explored both mouths of the Indus. The fleet, which was apparently to have sailed alongside him as he led his land forces westwards, was delayed by the monsoon, so that he and his men soon lost contact with the ships that were sailing under command of his admiral, Nearchus. Nearchus's crews were often terrified by the unfamiliar conditions of the

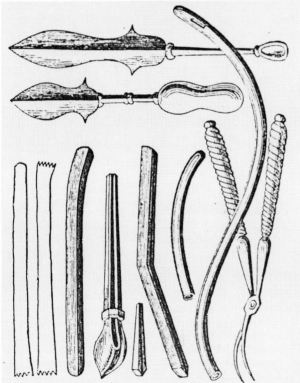

Even in the course of withdrawal, there was still fighting to be done, and dramatic events still occurred. Alexander was involved in fierce warfare against the Malli, a tribe of the Indus valley who had sympathized with the Cathaei. Impatient at the slow progress made by those of his men who

*This was Abreas; both Alexander's other rescuers, Peucestas and Leonnatus, were later promoted and decorated.

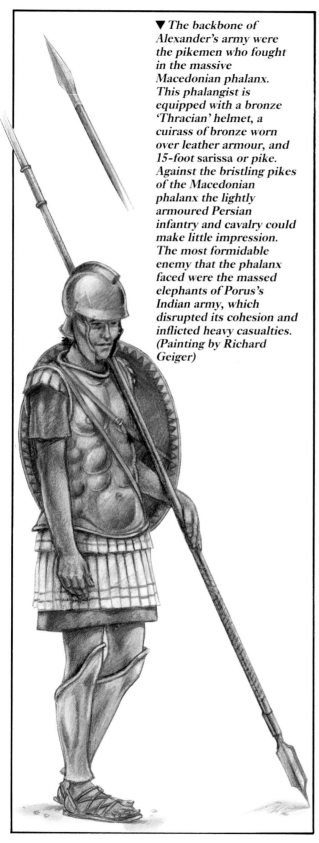

▼ The backbone of Alexander's army were the pikemen who fought in the massive Macedonian phalanx. This phalangist is equipped with a bronze 'Thracian' helmet, a cuirass of bronze worn over leather armour, and 15-foot sarissa or pike. Against the bristling pikes of the Macedonian phalanx the lightly armoured Persian infantry and cavalry could make little impression. The most formidable enemy that the phalanx faced were the massed elephants of Porus's Indian army, which disrupted its cohesion and inflicted heavy casualties. (Painting by Richard Geiger)

Indian Ocean, which included such phenomena as tides and whales. They underwent many privations and hardships, and some vessels were lost.

The land force suffered more horribly, as it wandered in the Gedrosian desert (modern Makran, still desolate). They at first trailed luxurious spoil acquired in their eastern wars, as well as women and children. But they had to burn the spoil, and they killed many of their pack animals for food. Although tortured by thirst, they met disaster in a torrent bed, where a meagre trickle of

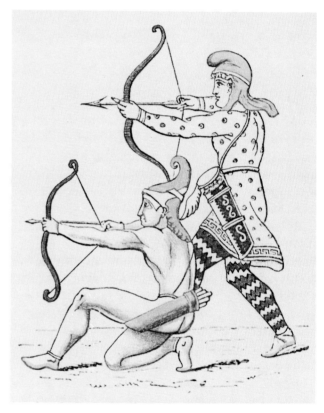

▲ The figure on the right is an Amazon as depicted on a Greek vase. The Amazons in Greek legend were a nation of women warriors who perpetuated their tribe by casual contact with neighbouring tribes. They were normally represented as dressed like Scythians, one of whom is here shown (copied from an Aeginetan marble) for the sake of comparison. Many legends cling to Alex-ander's eastern exploits, and he was reported to have encountered the Amazons during his campaigns. It is also related that a troop of armed women arrived in the Macedonian camp and that Alexander, feeling that their presence was prejudicial to good order and military discipline, sent them away with a promise that he would, as requested, visit their queen and get a child on her.

water had encouraged them to pitch camp – a sudden cloudburst over distant mountains turned the little stream without warning into a raging flood, and many of the women and children were drowned. There were considerable casualties both among men and animals during the march. The sick or exhausted were left to lie where they fell; none had the strength to help or carry them. When a violent wind obliterated all landmarks and effaced the tracks with sand, Alexander's guides, unable to read the stars, failed him. In this emergency, Alexander took charge personally and, using his sense of direction, led his desperate men back to the sea, where a fresh-water spring was discovered under the shingle beach. Sustained by a succession of such springs, they marched along the shore for seven days.

Alexander eventually made contact with Craterus inland, in Carmania (Kerman). Craterus brought him welcome pack-animals and elephants, and the remainder of the march was made under comparatively civilized conditions. At the entry of the Persian Gulf, Nearchus's men had fallen in with a Greek-speaking straggler from Alexander's army, and with a small party Nearchus himself ventured northward to meet Alexander.

After the inevitably emotional meeting, however, land and sea expeditions continued on separate lines. Nearchus sailed up the Persian Gulf, first to the mouth of the Euphrates, then to the Tigris, finally rejoining Alexander at Susa. Reports of the time taken by the historic voyage differ wildly. But it seems most likely that Nearchus sailed from the mouth of the Indus at the end of the south-westerly monsoons in October 325BC and reached Susa in spring 324.

In the last year of his life, Alexander faced a mutiny more serious than the passive resistance to which he had yielded on the Hyphasis. This occurred at Opis, some hundred miles north of Babylon. The dismissal of Macedonian veterans and the drafting of Persians into the phalanx had been extremely ill received. Alexander summarily executed the mutinous ringleaders and conciliated the rest with his ringing oratory. But his cosmopolitan attitudes and international policies remained everywhere a source of trouble. In his absence, there had been much evidence of

▲ The archer was the most common type of infantryman in the Indian army that faced Alexander. He was equipped with a large and powerful bamboo bow, as long as the archer was tall, and with a hemp or sinew string that could be drawn to the ear. Arrows were very long, of cane or reed and flighted with vulture feathers. Heads were usually of iron, sometimes of horn and, according to some Greek sources, could carry poison. Arrian says that the Indian bow was very powerful, no shield or cuirass being able to stop its arrows. Some of Alexander's officers maintain that it was too heavy to aim accurately, however, and the effects of Indian archery at the Hydaspes appear to have been negligible. (Painting by Richard Geiger)

corruption at the heart of his newly established empire. Harpalus, left in fiscal control, had been guilty of grave irregularities and absconded to Greece. Alexander's first impulse was to follow him and arrest him, but welcome news came that the fugitive had been murdered by his own subordinates.

Whatever the feelings of the Macedonians, Alexander certainly did not modify his plans for national fusion. He aimed not at a multi-racial society but at a fusion of culture, nation and race. In furtherance of this ideal, he obliged his Macedonian officers to marry oriental wives – nobody could say that he had not set an example himself. And he had decided to make Babylon the capital of his empire.

▲Alexander is sometimes portrayed wearing a lion's skin, and these illustrations based on ancient bronzes demonstrate the way in which a lion skin could be worn. Other animal skins were in fact used in the same way, the open jaws of the skin providing the orifice for the wearer's face. The ancient hero Heracles (Hercules) was often shown wearing a lion's skin. Alexander claimed to be a descendant of Heracles and was no doubt proud to dress like his ancestor.

In the later stages of his career, Alexander's character seems to have deteriorated, and he was more than ever liable to fits of caprice and self-indulgence, the vices the Greeks particularly associated with despotism. He also accepted the quasi-divine honours that were conferred on him by a flattering Greek deputation. Perhaps his divine aspirations had been stimulated even at an earlier date on the occasion of his visit to the Libyan oracle of Ammon.

The fame of his eastern conquests had extended even to the western Mediterranean, and while near Babylon in 324 he was honoured by friendly embassies from Libya, Carthage, Spain and Gaul. Perhaps if he had lived longer he would have turned his thoughts to *western* conquest, but at this time he was planning an expedition into Arabia, inspired evidently by Nearchus's reconnaissance.

His preparations, particularly in the construction of a fleet for operations in the Persian Gulf, were cut short by his death which followed a sudden fever, in 323BC. He named no successor. It was not the first time that his life had been threatened by sickness or wounds, and on these former occasions he had shown no inclination to name a successor. Death in battle had in fact threatened him continuously, yet the prospect had never apparently fixed his thoughts on the question of succession. According to Arrian he was speechless in the last twenty-four hours of his life, but Curtius represents him as speaking coherently to within moments of his death. Either he did not wish to indicate a successor or he was indifferent. In the upshot, his senior officers parcelled his vast empire among themselves and their own successors, who, as flamboyant warlords, continued to fight each other throughout the next two centuries. It was possibly something Alexander had foreseen and to which he was resigned.

Perhaps politics were not even his ultimate consideration. The last years of his life shed a new light on his character, and we may see him as an obsessive explorer who fought his way across the world because this was the only possible way of exploring it. His enemies were simply those who tried to prevent him from going where he liked when he liked.

AFTER ALEXANDER

Philip Arrhidaeus, Alexander's half-brother, who had probably accompanied the army to Asia Minor in 334BC, was in Babylon at the time of Alexander's death. The son of Philip II and his Thessalian mistress Philinna, Arrhidaeus was generally recognized as lawful successor to the throne of Macedon, though his power was merely nominal. He was in fact simple-minded, a political asset to anyone who could claim to be his guardian. Eventually he fell into the hands of Olympias, Alexander's mother, who, jealous for her own posterity, put him to death in 317BC.

Alexander's posthumous son by Roxana, still a child, then remained king as Alexander IV of Macedon. But he and his mother were murdered in 310 by Cassander, son of the regent Antipater (who had died in 319). Cassander, ruthlessly ridding himself of all possible rivals, saw himself as the obvious heir to the Macedonian throne.

If Alexander's family did not inherit Macedon, neither did Macedon inherit the Persian Empire. The western territories conquered by Alexander were, by 321BC, under the control of Antigonus, originally Alexander's governor in Phrygia (northwest Asia Minor). Antigonus regarded himself as sole heir to the whole of Alexander's empire and quickly suppressed two of Alexander's officers who disputed his claim. His was the strongest of the successor kingdoms, and there now arose a combination of the other rulers against him: Seleucus, who governed the East from Babylon: Ptolemy, who now ruled Egypt; Cassander in Macedon; and Lysimachus in Thrace.

This powerful alliance produced the defeat and death of Antigonus at Ipsus in Phrygia in 301BC. The result was that the successor kingdoms remained separate until the second century BC, when one by one they fell under the power of Rome, the last representative of Macedonian dynastic rule being the famed Cleopatra, beloved

▲ *The coin here shown is a tetradrachm of Seleucus I, who had been prominent among Alexander's senor officers and fought at the Hydaspes. The helmet is an elaborate type of Attic helmet and covers the ears. The cheek-pieces in such helmets may or may not have been movable. In Alexander's day, more open kinds of helmet were commonly adopted to facilitate vision and hearing. The reverse shows a winged Victory crowning a trophy of arms and armour.*

of Julius Caesar and Mark Antony, who committed suicide in 30BC.

The Macedonian domination of north-west India did not long survive the withdrawal of Alexander. The Punjab was soon overrun by Chadragupta Maurya, the Indian king known to the Greeks as Sandrakottos. However, as the Mauryan power declined, India was again conquered by Greek-speaking kings who were the successors of Alexander's governors and garrisons in Bactria and Afghanistan. They penetrated as far as the Ganges valley, though they never consolidated their conquests so far east.

Coins inscribed doubly in Greek and Indian scripts are evidence of some forty Indo-Greek kings during the third and second centuries BC. One of them, Menander, who ruled from 155 to 130BC, survives in Indian tradition as Milinda, a wise and just monarch, who was converted to Buddhism.

▲ Silver tetradrachms of this type were issued by the first Ptolemy of Egypt. Ptolemy, as one of Alexander's senior officers, succeeded to the governorship of Egypt at Alexander's death. He, like Seleucus, was with Alexander at the battle of the Hydaspes and had triumphed over Porus' elephants. His coin, here shown, still bears the name 'Alexander' on the reverse. On the obverse, the helmet, formed like an elephant's head, is clearly reminiscent of the lion-mask trophy of Heracles, which appears so often in Alexander's coinage. The curling ram's horn of Ammon, Alexander's personal badge, is also present. Perhaps we should see in the sinuous poise of the elephant's trunk a reminder of the cobra emblem on a Pharaoh's brow.

▲ This square silver coin is inscribed in Greek with the name of Apollodotus Soter. The reverse carries an Asiatic script. Apollodotus was a Greek king of the Bactrian dynasty which, following in the footsteps of Alexander the Great, invaded India in the second century BC. History tells us very little about the Greek monarchs who inherited Alexander's conquests in the far east of the Persian Empire; our knowledge, such as it is, is mostly derived from their coinage.

GLOSSARY

In the present book, glossary words have been avoided so far as possible, but below will be found a short list of words, transliterated from Greek, which the reader may meet in this or other books about Alexander. Singular forms are for the most part given, but plurals in 'oi' or 'ai' are easy to recognize. One must also be prepared for Latin forms, in which 'os', 'oi', 'a' and 'ai' become 'us', 'i', 'e' and 'ae' respectively. Also, 'Parmenio' and 'Aristo' are alternatives for the Greek 'Parmenion' and 'Ariston'. Greek 'ei' Latinizes as 'i'. So one will find 'Clitus' as well as 'Cleitos', also often (regrettably) 'Cleitus'. The letter 'y' was used in Latin to render the Greek letter 'upsilon' (originally pronounced thinly like a French 'u'), but occasionally 'u' replaces 'y' in English transliterations. Some proper names are regularly Anglicized. 'Agrianes' (four syllables with short 'e') may be represented in English books as 'Agrianians', or 'Malli' ('oi') as Mallians. Philip is of course English for 'Philippus' ('os') and Alexander is English or Latin for 'Alexandros'. Greek names transliterated from works in other languages (especially guide books) may bear traces of the original. More often than English, German reflects the Greek form and spelling, preferring 'k' to Latin 'c'. The French Gallicize more frequently than we Anglicize, writing not only 'Alexandre' and 'Philippe', but 'Démosthènes' (three syllables) and 'Néarque' – not to mention 'Macédoine'. Incidentally, 'Macedon' in English refers more particularly to the political state, 'Macedonia' to the territory or later Roman province. 'Makedon', in Greek, is a Macedonian.

Agēma	Vanguard. 'Basilikon agēma' (= Royal Vanguard), usually of cavalry, but also of hypaspists (see below).
Akontion	Javelin.
Basilikoi Paides	'Royal lads', a kind of OTC, which followed the Macedonian kings on active service. Often translated 'Royal Pages'. They are known chiefly for their plot against Alexander's life in Bactria.
Chiliarchia	A unit of a thousand men; a 'chiliarchy'.
Chiliarchēs	Commander of a 'chiliarchy'; also used of a Persian king's prime minister.
Hetairos	A Companion. The Companions were an élite body of cavalry led by the Macedonian kings. Sometimes they appear as 'philoi' in Greek and are translated into English as 'Friends'.
Hipparchia	Latterly a subdivision of the Companions. Its numerical strength seems to have varied.
Hipparchos	Commander of a hipparchia ('hipparchy').
Hoplitēs	Greek infantryman, carrying round flanged shield; a 'hoplite'.
Hypaspistēs	A Macedonian infantryman armed with spear and conspicuous shield, a 'hypaspist'. The hypaspists were latterly referred to as the 'silver-shields'. They are often translated as the 'Guards'.
Ilē	Squadron of cavalry.
Ilarchēs	The commander of an 'ilē'.
Kopis	A slashing sword, with curved blade, distinct from the straight, two-edged, pointed 'xiphos'.
Lochos	A company, subdivision of an 'ilē'.

Longchē	A spear, shorter than a 'sarissa' (see below).	Sarissophoros	Lancer. In the Macedonian army (= prodromos = lancer scout).
Machaira	A slashing sword (= kopis).		
Mēlophoroi	'Apple-bearers', Greek word for Persian royal guard with ball-pommels on their spears.	Satrapēs	'Satrap', Greek form of Persian word meaning provincial governor.
Peltē	(or 'pelta') A small, light shield of skin or wicker.	Stadion	'Stade'. Variable Greek measure of about 600 feet.
Peltastēs	Originally, a light-armed skirmisher, with pelta, but in the later fourth century often more heavily equipped.	Somatophylax	(plural somatophylakes) Bodyguard.
		Synaspismos	Close formation of the phalanx, 'shield to shield'; often translated 'locked shields'.
Pentekontoros	A fifty-oared galley.		
Pentērēs	Quinquereme; galley with five rowers each side in each section.	Taxis	Military unit in a general sense, but regularly applied to units of infantry in particular; often translated 'battalion'.
Pezetairos	Macedonian infantryman. 'Asthetairoi' were those recruited from the towns rather than the rural localities.	Tetrērēs	Quadrireme; galley with four rowers on each side in each section.
Phalanx	Line of battle, line of infantry, used specially in modern accounts to denote the dense Macedonian pike line.	Thorax	Cuirass
		Triakontoros	Thirty-oared galley.
		Triērēs	Trireme; galley with three rowers on each side in each section.
Prodromos	Scout (= sarissophoros, i.e., lancer scout).		
Sarissa	Infantry pike or cavalry lance. (More strictly: 'sarīsa')	Xyston	Lance.

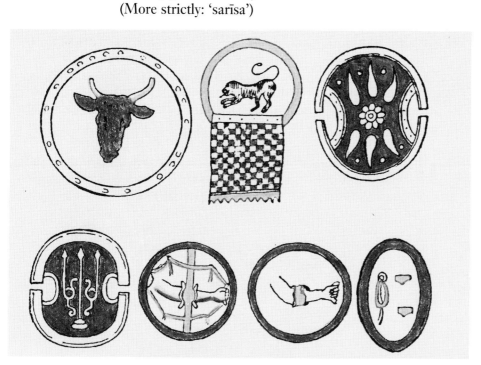

◀ *Greek and Macedonian shields – apart from some bronze fittings, were made of perishable materials, but our knowledge of them is widely based on surviving representations. The Macedonian shield was smaller and lighter than that of the Greek hoplite. It was supported by means of a forearm bracket and probably a strap round the neck and shoulder. Both hands were thus left free to manage the Macedonian pike (sarissa).*

THE BATTLEFIELDS TODAY

No matter which Turkish river you identify as the Granicus, the village of Dimetoka is probably close to the site of the battle. A traveller arriving in Istanbul by air may also visit the Istambul Museum, which contains the famous Alexander sarcophagus with sculptured reliefs perhaps representing the Granicus battle. It should be noticed that Erdek – a quiet Turkish tourist resort on the south Marmara coast – is five hours distant by sea or road from Istanbul; Dimetoka is about 35 miles west of Erdek.

The battle of Issus was fought in what is now a small Turkish administrative district (isanjakl), named Iskanderun after its chief town, a seaport near the Syrian frontier. 'Iskander' is both Turkish and Arabic for Alexander – hence the name. Iskanderun, previously known in the west as Alexandretta, was the city Alexander founded after his Issus campaign. The battlefield of Issus lies about twenty miles farther north, probably on the River Payas – the Pinarus of our ancient texts. But Payas or Pinarus, the river's course has inevitably changed since 333BC, and so has the adjacent coastline.

Tyre is on the southern coast of Lebanon. It is now no longer an island, being united with the mainland on the sector where Alexander's mole was built. There are many ancient ruins both on the original island and on the mainland coast, but these are not survivals of the Phoenician city that resisted Alexander; most are of Roman or Byzantine date. In more peaceful times, Tyre could be approached either from Beirut or from Israel. Our present suggestion is that the visit should be postponed.

With regard to Gaugamela, one notes that Baghdad is an international airport. It is connected by rail with Mosul and (over a metre-gauge track) with Kirkuk and Arbil (Arbela). Tel Gomel, which has been identified with Gaugamela, the site of Alexander's victory, lies about twenty miles north-east of Mosul. Approach to the battlefield would be made easier by a knowledge of Arabic. At the time of writing, difficulty may be experienced in obtaining an entry visa for Iraq or Syria.

The landmarks of Alexander's Indian campaigns are located with misleading precision by some writers. The rivers of the Punjab have wandered widely in their courses since Alexander's day, with resulting transformations of terrain. The whole area now lies within Pakistan. Tourism has been enthusiastically developed here, and Taxila with its important archaeological museum may be reached from Rawalpindi by mini-bus. Rawalpindi itself is in the heart of the 'Alexander country'. Islamabad-Rawalpindi is a major Pakistani airport, second only to the international air-junction of Karachi.

Please note that all reasonable care has been taken to check the accuracy of the above information at the time of writing (January 1990). Beyond that, no guarantee can he given.

CHRONOLOGY

336BC   **June:** Assassination of Philip. Alexander's accession.
Autumn: Alexander dictates in Greece.

335   **Spring and autumn:** War against the Balkan tribes.
October: Destruction of Thebes.

334   **May:** The crossing of the Hellespont.
May or June: The Battle of the Granicus.
Later summer: Occupation of the Greek Asiatic cities. Sieges of Miletus and Halicarnassus.

353   **June:** Death of Memnon.
April to July: Alexander's reconnaissance at Gordium.
November: The Battle of Issus.

332   **January to July:** Siege of Tyre.
September to November: Siege of Gaza.
December: Entry into Egypt.

331   **July to September:** March to the Euphrates. Crossing of the Tigris.
1 October: The Battle of Gaugamela. Flight of Darius.

330   **January to May:** The occupation of Mesopotamia and Babylonia.
May: Defeat of Agis by Antipater at Megalopolis.
July: Pursuit and death of Darius.
October: Execution of Philotas and murder of Parmenio.

329   **Summer:** Capture of Bessus.

328   **Winter:** Defeat and death of Spitamenes.

327-6   **Winter:** Campaign in north-west India. Hephaestion on the Indus.

326   **May:** The Battle of the Hydaspes.
Summer: Advance to the Hyphasis and withdrawal.

326-25   **Winter:** War against the Malli. Alexander recovers from an almost fatal wound.

325   **February:** Alexander assembles his forces on the Indus.
June: Craterus marches westward.
Late August: Alexander marches westward.
October: Nearchus sails westward.
December: Reunion with Craterus in Carmania.

324   **January:** Reunion with Nearchus in Carmania.
February: Second reunion with Nearchus at the head of the Persian Gulf.
Summer: Mutiny at Opis.
Autumn: Hephaestion's death. Alexander at Ecbatana.

323   **April to May:** Alexander joins the main army at Babylon.
10 June: Death of Alexander at Babylon.

A GUIDE TO FURTHER READING

1. Easily accessible translations of the ancient texts

I. The Loeb Classical Library (Text and translation):
ARRIAN. *History of Alexander and Indica*, 2 vols, P. A. Brunt (1976, 1983). Contains a 75-page introduction and 28 appendixes. The earlier Loeb text and translation by E. Iliff Robson has been revised.
CURTIUS Q. *History of Alexander*, 2 vols, J. C. Rolfe.
DIODORUS SICULUS (12 vols), vol. VIII, C. B. Welles (1963).
PLUTARCH. *Parallel Lives* (11 vols, 1914–26) vol. VII, B. Perrin.

II. Penguin Classics (Editor Betty Radice):
ARRIAN. *The Campaigns of Alexander*, translated by Aubrey de Sélincourt. Revised with new introduction and notes by J. R. Hamilton, 1971.
PLUTARCH 'The Age of Alexander' in *Nine Greek Lives*, translated and annotated by Ian Scott Kilvert; introduction by G. T. Griffith (1973).
CURTIUS, QUINTUS RUFUS. *The History of Alexander*, translated by John Yardley with an introduction and notes by Waldemar Heckel (1984).

III. There is no easily accessible English translation of JUSTIN, but that used for reference by Professor N. G. L. Hammond (see below) is by J. S. Watson in the Bohn Library Edition.

2. Modern studies

Many valuable contributions to the subject, including notably those of E. Badian, are in periodical publications, but the following English books are often cited in studies of Alexander.
FULLER, J. F. C. *The Generalship of Alexander the Great*, London, 1958. Da Capo reprint of New Brunswick edition, 1960.

FOX, R. LANE. *Alexander the Great*, London, 1973, 1978; 28 plates, 7 maps.
GREEN, P. *Alexander the Great*, London, 1970; paperback 1974; handsomely illustrated.
HAMMOND, N. G. L. *Alexander the Great: king, commander and statesman*, London, 1981; 2nd ed. Bristol 1989. Listed references provide a useful bibliography.
MARSDEN, E. W. *The Campaign of Gaugamela*, Liverpool, 1964; Objective scholarship with map, diagrams, tables, and numerical estimates.
PEARSON L. *The Lost Histories of Alexander the Great*, New York, 1960; for those who study the ancient sources.
TARN, W. W. *Alexander the Great*, 2 vols, Cambridge, 1948; the account is highly favourable to Alexander.
WILCKEN, U. *Alexander the Great*, translation by G. C. Richards, London, 1932; New York, ed. E. Borza, 1967. A balanced view. Borza's bibliography concentrates on works published since the original appearance of Wilcken's book and includes many works in periodical publications.

3. Books with relevant chapters and/or illustrations

CONNOLLY, P. *The Greek Armies*, Macdonald, 1977.
KEEGAN, J. *The Mask of Command*, London, 1987; paperback 1989.
MARSDEN, E. W. *Greek and Roman Artillery*, Oxford, 1969.
PARKE, H. W. *Greek Mercenary Soldiers from the Earliest Times to the Battle of Ipsus*, Oxford, 1933.
SNODGRASS, A. M. *Arms and Armour of the Greeks*, London, 1967; reprint 1982.
WARRY, J. *Warfare in the Classical World*, London, 1980, and New York, 1981.

INDEX

(References to illustrations are shown in **bold**. Plates are shown with page and caption locators in brackets.)